To Ken Gross
May you be eternally blessed

FAITH
VS.
FATE

The Shaun Stephenson Story

**From Undocumented Live-in Nanny & Maid To
Director with Pre-Paid Legal Services Incorporated**

FAITH VS. FATE

The Shaun Stephenson Story

**From Undocumented Live-in Nanny & Maid To
Director with Pre-Paid Legal Services Incorporated**

HAROLD A. BASCOM

Caribbean Writers Series Novelist

&

SHAUN STEPHENSON

KOKER PRESS

Hackensack, New Jersey

Library of Congress Control Number: 2007909971
ISBN-13: 978-0-9802063-0-2
ISBN-10: 0-9802063-0-8

Published by KOKER PRESS
145 Union Street
Hackensack, New Jersey 07601-4119

The book, *FAITH Vs. FATE, The Shaun Stephenson Story,* may be purchased in quantity at special discounts. Please contact KOKER Press at the above address, or Email a request to either of the following addresses, haroldbantu@aol.com or shaun6@comcast.net, Subject line: FAITH VS. FATE COPIES.

Back Cover Photo © 2007 Keiko El
Author Photo © 2007 Parry Bancroft

*This book I dedicate to my mother, Jean Harry
whose pain opened my eyes to life.*

Contents

CONTENTS *(continued)*

CONTENTS *(continued)*

FOREWORD

By David Smile

Mr. David Smile is an Executive Director, Platinum-Jacket Earner, and Million-Dollar Inductee with Pre-Paid Legal Services Incorporated.

In November 1953, Queen Elizabeth II, visited Jamaica, and my dad took me downtown to Kingston to see her. He lifted me onto his shoulders to see over the crowd, and she was in this magnificent car that was silver and gleaming gray with white-wall tires, and the chrome parts glinted under the sun...

"What kind of car is that, Daddy?" I asked.

My dad replied, proud of his knowledge: "That's a Rolls Royce, David... —the Rolls Royce Silver Cloud. That's a car for the rich people, boy..."

And below the clamor of the cheering crowd I said to myself, "I am going to own a Rolls Royce when I grow up!" And one of my many dreams was born; in my mind nothing was going to stop me from one day owning a Rolls Royce.

One of my pastimes as a boy back in Jamaica was watching the planes leave as I sat in the fork of an *ackee* tree... and in that tree I used to dream of being in America with my mother where the streets were paved with gold.

As I read *FAITH VS. FATE*—the part where Shaun Stephenson emerges from the JFK arrivals lounge with only the clothes on her back and a dream—I remembered my own arrival as a kid, at that very airport. It was the Idlewild Airport then... and it had snowed that day, but in my mind I was determined to see the gold that covered the ground. When I got off the plane, I stooped to the airport's tarmac and brushed away the white stuff to see the precious metal beneath.

Amusing stuff, I know, but there was still my dream to be wealthy enough to own a Rolls Royce, and I told myself that I *knew* how I'd get rich: I was going to get an education and my

xi

dream would come through. And in time I went to high school and then to university, became very qualified, and found a great nine-to-five job in the banking industry. But still I couldn't afford to buy that Rolls Royce. Truth was, with my nine-to-five job I couldn't even afford to buy the grill of such a car.

But by and by I discovered direct sales and was able to realize that dream: I bought my first Rolls Royce at age 23. Through commitment, hope and with faith, I was able to realize many golden moments in my life: At age 26 I was running a successful seminar company which, in 1971, made a before-tax profit of six million dollars.

But I would be lying if I told you that everything for me was all rosy from then on; it was not. I suffered a huge financial failure at the stock market and lost everything. I was wiped out —facilitating the need to restart from the bottom. I was broke I had to borrow two hundred and forty nine dollars from my partner, and with that, I took advantage of the opportunity that Mr. Harland Stonecipher has created and became an Independent Associate with Pre-Paid Legal Services Incorporated. I dared to dream as Shaun Stephenson dreams in this book, and as a result of my commitment to that dream I am now an Executive Director, a platinum Jacket Earner, and a million-dollar inductee with Paid legal Services.

Like me, and like many other immigrants who started with just a dream, Shaun Stephenson is on a journey —a quest to succeed, and she will. Why? Because of her belief in the direct-selling industry... because of her commitment... and because of her faith.

PROLOGUE: 2007

Interview with Stanley El

EDITED 2007 RADIO INTERVIEW TRANSCRIPT:

Voices of school children: "I pledge allegiance to the flag of the United States of America, and to the Republic for which it stands, one Nation under God, indivisible, with liberty and justice for all."

"And Welcome again to the "American Dream" ... I am Stanley El... and Alex Grisco —and our guest Shaun Stephenson... —how you doing, Shaun?"

"I'm awesome... —extraordinary!"

"You know that's the word, right? —Absolutely extraordinary.... Shaun! ... It's been a while?"

"It has been."

"You've been here —gosh! —How many years ago?"

"03 —could we count? —Three, four, five —four years?"

"Four years...

"Shaun, why don't you begin by giving us some kind of background, you know —where you're from —grew up?"

"Okay... actually I'm originally from South America... from a country called Guyana—not Ghana—so I'm not African... I came here —this year it's going to be fourteen years, and I came here with a dream like many other immigrants do... I started out here as a nanny taking care of five children even though I've not had formal training in childcare. Other than my little cousins I've taken care of —no such background..."

"What were you in your country?"

"I was a librarian and then I worked for one of the largest hotels in my country as a front office manager..."

"Uh huh..."

"My last job before I came to here was a loans representative of our National Bank..."

"And then you came to America and began as a nanny...

"Now... have you been back to Guyana since?"

"Yes, I've been back, but after I came here it had been five years before I returned home... it had been five years I hadn't seen my family. My husband—who was my fiancé then—didn't see me for five years... —we talked on the phone a lot, so we both ended up with huge phone bills. ... In ninety-eight I finally went back —but not back to Guyana. I met him halfway on an island called Trinidad —neutral ground, so we could have seen whether we still loved each other..."

"Neutral ground... Trinidad is a nice place for that. I hear it's beautiful down there... —Now you're here, and you've been here a while... —What would be your American dream, Shaun?"

"It's huge..."

CHAPTER 1: 2007
Oklahoma

REFLECTIONS ON GUYANA, SOUTH AMERICA
WHERE AN AMERICAN VISA IS GOLD

Alleged lines from a letter written by a father, newly arrived in America, to his daughter back in his country: "My dear daughter... this place America is heaven!"

MARCH. Oklahoma, Oklahoma City. It had been a long day. Shaun Stephenson, nee Harry stood unwinding on the balcony outside of the Best Western Hotel room in which she stayed with her mom and aunt. They were in *the Sooner State* with over twelve thousand others in attendance of the Pre Paid Legal Services' two-day Annual Convention. In Shaun's heart, the day at the Convention replayed... the new associates she met, the friendly executives, the collective euphoria of positivism and hope —the camaraderie: It had been a good day.

She stood on the balcony from her room and looked down at the rectangular patch of still, aquamarine water. Along its longest sides the ever-present poolside chairs were arrayed. Stylized lamps glowed at points on the walls enclosing the deserted pool area. The beach umbrellas that seemed to grow from the round, glazed tables positioned about, were closed. There were no swimmers, only the pool... tranquil like Shaun's mind as she breathed easily... so calm in her psyche. She closed her eyes.

Her thoughts were miles away... thousands of transatlantic miles away and back to the Northern regions of South America where Guyana her homeland lay close to the vast Atlantic Ocean and the Caribbean Sea. She was remembering the day she stood outside the U.S. Embassy in Duke Street, Georgetown, quietly awaiting her turn to be interviewed; and quietly awaiting her fate, she had prayed.

Is today the first day of my destiny?

She stood before the window where the Consular Officer waited with piercing blue eyes, and a rather unusual physiological challenge presented itself: remembering how to breathe calmly.

"What is your career plan?

"What are you doing now—in terms of employment?

"Do you plan to remain in banking?

"What plans do you have for the future?

"How long do you wish to stay in the United States?

"When do you plan on returning to Guyana? ..."

She had been prepared and mixed truth and half-truths skillfully. In the end she convinced him that she was going to return and not destined to be yet another of the tens-of-thousands never to honor the granted temporary visa. She was asked to come back to the Embassy in order to pick up her passport that she had obtained some seven years ago. In her heart she knew that one day she was going to be able to travel to the United States.

With her eyes closed above the swimming pool in Oklahoma City, it all came back. It was more than half an hour of interconnected streets back to the Guyana National Cooperative Bank where she worked as a loans rep. She walked, as if on air, back to the office. Earlier that morning she had sent a message with a co-worker to let her boss, Mrs. Sinclair, know that she would be running late for work —that there was something she had to do before she reported in. Mrs. Sinclair had no idea of the business Shaun had to tend to. When she came in, at about midmorning, her boss looked at her, smiled and said. "You are glowing —happy... —want to share something with me?"

Anita Sinclair was a professional woman with a calm air of efficiency, but yet she was ever pleasant to her staff... so unassuming... so kind. Shaun told her what had transpired and Mrs. Sinclair expressed gladness for Shaun that seemed genuine. "You have to return later to pick up your passport with the visa stamped into it," she said.

"Yes —at four this afternoon..."

"Don't worry —I'm going to let you leave early, and I'll wait until you return, okay? I'm so excited for you, Shaun..."

"I'm so excited for myself, Mrs. Sinclair... thank you ..."

"I won't lie, Shaun!" one of her co-workers in the loans department said to her, "I envy you... this is your opportunity to see the last of this blighted place!"

Another said, "God knows how much you deserve this, Shaun. This day, I guess, was long in coming. But it's here... Just don't forget us!"

It was not the first time she had tried to acquire a visa to the United States of America. A couple of years earlier she had actually paid a lump-sum of money to a guy who had convinced her that he had 'links' in the U.S. Embassy and could have gotten her one. In the end she got conned —lost her money and lost the trust of even her relatives whom she had convinced that a visa to the great land of opportunity would be in her passport.

She sat at her desk and time dragged slowly. She was going to leave for the Embassy soon. It was years after the visa fiasco, and the promise of a visa was now official. She sat at her desk and refused to entertain any doubts —fears that when she got back to the Embassy anything would be amiss. She was a girl on a mission; there would only be one outcome for her this day: her visa to the United States of America.

When she got there at four that afternoon, a five-year multiple visa was stamped into her passport. She passed her fingers gently over the seal... ever so gently over the seal of the most powerful country on the face of God's earth and a slight tremor rippled in her sternum. *Oh my God it is real!! I have a visa to go to America!* She shouted with joy from every pore of her body; she rediscovered true happiness and containing —concealing her deep excitement was a huge task but she succeeded. She struck out for the office where her boss waited. When she got there they celebrated modestly, and then it was time to go home to Carlton, the man with whom she lived. She called him 'Doods," and he called her, 'Babes.'

She joined the huge ferry that took her to Vreed-en-Hoop— translated from Dutch to mean *Peace-and-Hope*—and she too floated. In her heart she was eager to tell —eager to shout to him even before she entered their home over in the country separated from Georgetown City where she worked, by a wide, muddy river with the name Demerara... but she knew she shouldn't because he wouldn't believe her.

When she went home to her man and told him by-the-way-sort of, he did not believe. She was not surprised. He, like many others did not let her live down the last time she was burned by a visa scam artist. But she knew what she knew.

That evening she looked around the house in which she lived with Carlton and his mother. In her heart she knew that soon she would be saying goodbye to the old house... —goodbye to every hole in the roof, to every hole in the floor... —goodbye to the muddy yard, the stand pipe at the front and the dusty public road that ran by... goodbye to the pit latrine aback with the maggots and dirty water that jumped and touched her bottoms... goodbye to the bathroom in the yard that forced her to take baths when it grew dark. She knew she would soon be saying goodbye to the poverty from which she had always fought to detangle herself.

She knew too, that soon she would be saying goodbye to Carlton with whom she'd been since she was only thirteen... with whom she became a woman... with whom she lost her first child.

She knew however, that once she was in America things would be better for her, for Carlton, and for everyone she cared for. It was going to be her big break and through it she would lead many from a wilderness of economic bondage to America... *The Promised Land.*

With eyes closed above the swimming pool in Oklahoma City, it all came back to Shaun Stephenson, citizen of the United States, and Certified Identity Theft Risk Management Specialist with the Pre Paid Legal Services Incorporated entity.

The first person she called overseas was her Aunt Claudette who lived in Plainfield, New Jersey.

"Aunt Claudette! —I got through! —I got through! —I got the visa!"

"Which Visa, Shaun?"

"I went in to the Embassy and they gave me a five-year multiple visa! ... Aunt Claudette? —You there?"

"Yes, I'm here, but the news have me speechless —I-I'm so happy for you, Shaun..."

"So, Aunt Claudette —how soon can I come? Once you tell me I'll hand in my resignation at the bank! ... —It won't be any problem!"

"Well... —Let me talk to your Uncle Gavin and see how things can happen. I'm only now getting my traveling documents in order—you know..."

"Okay..."

"I'll be coming home this summer and you can come back with me to the States —how that sounds?"

"That sounds good, Aunt Claudette!"

"I'm so happy for you, Shaun..."

But it wasn't until four months later that her Aunt Claudette was able to return to Guyana with her American-born son Gavin, and when she did, it was a grand family reunion.

At the end of her Aunt Claudette's stay, Shaun would be returning with her to Plainfield, New Jersey where she would help in a family business owned by her aunt's husband. At last! Shaun was going to be leaving for America with her Aunt Claudette. This had ever been little Shaun's dream... a dream so special as far back as she could have remembered.

CHAPTER 2: 1993

New York to New Jersey

REFLECTIONS ON ARRIVAL

Give me your tired, your poor,
Your huddled masses yearning to breathe free,
The wretched refuse of your teeming shore,
Send these, the homeless, tempest-tossed to me,
I lift my lamp beside the golden door!

—*Emma Lazarus, New York City, 1883*

On the evening of September, 3rd, 1993 Shaundal Michelle Myanda Harry, a twenty-three-year-old loans representative from Guyana, South America, deplanes at John F. Kennedy International Airport with her young cousin and Aunt Claudette. Anxiety plagues her as she waits before the immigration officer who processes her papers.

How long will she give me?

Shaun's armed with a five-year multiple visa; but how long would she be allowed to stay on this her first trip to America? The sound of her heart resonates in her head as she breathes evenly, carefully —trying not to project her anxiety. Back at the Georgetown Embassy she had told the Consular Officer that she needed to go on a two-week vacation to America, but in her heart she knew that she would return only after she became a Resident Alien in the great U.S. of A.

Please God! —Let it be at least one month!

At last the Immigration officer is finished. She looks levelly into the eyes of Shaundal Stephenson clad in a red blazer over a black and red top... black skirt, and standing five feet seven. The Immigration woman smiles cordially.

Shaun's lucky: six months!

She emerges with her cousin Gavin and her Aunt Claudette

into the arrivals lounge and in her mind she exults: *I am here! Here in America! What do I have? Just these clothes on my back and a dream... but that's okay. I am here!*

. . .

A light breeze ruffled her hair as she stood on the balcony outside of her Best Western Hotel room. She remembered the day she arrived in America... the calm that overtook her when her Cousin Wennie, his wife Joanna, and their daughter met them and led the way to the waiting Lincoln, Town Car.

Shaun remembered that calm —destined to be that symbolical stillness before a storm of new experiences to come her way. In her mind, however, there was a sigh of relief after a very trying life back in her country: She had left behind so many years of struggle and pain and hope. There had always been faith, however. But though Guyana was behind her, she knew she could never forget it —turn her back on the land where her umbilical cord was buried. The friends she had left behind was Guyana; her brother Glen whom she had left behind was Guyana; her parents whom she had left behind was Guyana; Carlton's mom who loved her like a daughter was Guyana. And then there was Carlton himself... the man she knew that she would one day marry... He too was Guyana, but so much more.

At last she was in the land of opportunity! —At last she was where she had dreamt of being ever since she was a child fascinated by the beautiful little dresses 'Auntie Claudette' sent her from America.

The trip from the airport to her aunt's home is an archived memory. Her cousin's car with its tray of glasses and refreshments felt like a little hotel room on wheels wending its way through the streets of Queens, Brooklyn, Manhattan, and towards the Holland Tunnel. When they emerged, Shaun experienced an interconnecting complexity of highways and expressways that took them through cityscapes, industrialized factoryscapes, suburban landscapes, urban jungles of brownstone, and more industrialized landscapes... and when the town car finally exited its last highway, her aunt muttered that they would soon be home.

At last they swung into Plainfield, New Jersey's Compton

Avenue. Many trees were interspersed with the elegant Colonial styled houses all along it. As the lawns, flower gardens, and beautiful fences —hedges slipped by, Shaun felt at home. The apparent cleanliness of the street amazed her. It was as if out of a movie.

But the trees... she kept being drawn back to the trees. *Something is wrong with them,* she thought.

At last they pulled up before a huge Victorian house —in her mind a mansion painted in a hue of cream.

"Well my niece... this *my* home ..." her Aunt Claudette said proudly. "This is where I live..."

Shaun stepped out of the long car and looked around... "Aunt Claudette..." she said. "Why are the leaves falling? —Are the trees dying?"

Shaun smiled as she remembered her unfamiliarity of seasonal changes in North America. It was soon to be fall and her fortunes were destined to be as variable as the colors of autumn leaves.

. . .

She opened her eyes, took a deep breath and looked at her watch next to the gold band that her mother-in-law had given her: It is twelve midnight. Tomorrow the Pre-Paid legal Services Convention continued. She needed to rest. She turned away from the pool and entered her hotel room where her aunt and mother snored lightly in rounds.

The Best Western hotel room in which they stayed was modest but very comfortable. The calm color of its walls complimented the way she felt. Off to her left was a simple chair-table arrangement. She rested her bag down, sat, took off her heels and massaged her Achilles tendons as she looked at her mom fondly.

Her mom... She had brought her mom to America and was happy she did. Back in Guyana her mom had a very trying life. In Shaun's heart, her father never treated her mother right... never showed her that he cared. She looked at her sleeping and was reminded that indeed there were angels but not necessarily blond-haired, blue-eyed, and with wings. They came with every color of skin there are, and her mom was one that suffered because she loved a man who didn't love her back.

Shaun sighed away the memory of her mom's trying times. "Oh well, she's okay now," she whispered and walked carefully to the upper right-hand corner of the room where a porcelain sink waited below a simple mirror. There she allowed herself a brief moment of narcissism. She felt proud of the woman who looked back at her... a modest, beautiful woman, who didn't think she was all that, smiled back... a simple, unpretentious woman with the aura of a pre-school teacher... a woman who granted no credibility to the 'greed-is-good' philosophy... a connector... a builder of relationships... a woman who held to a mission of freely giving to the world.

She went into the bathroom. She yawned and thought of Carlton her husband so many miles away in Mantua, New Jersey. *Is he okay?* She had always been supportive of Carlton's dreams... his aspirations, but now it seems her aspirations —her growth as a Pre-Paid Legal Director and businesswoman, threatened their marriage. She had hoped that they might have grown together —walked hand in hand into a glowing future together: him the successful graphic artist and writer; she the entrepreneur.

"Maybe it's not to be," she whispered as she sat on the bed separated from the one in which her aunt and mom slept, by a nightstand with a lamp that rose from it. She gazed emptily at the floral design on the lampshade. *Is my love for him enough to fix things between us?*

There is so much she wished he understood about her —that as much as she loved him, she was not going to give in to being less than what she knew in her gut that she could yet be. "I will try to keep our marriage, together!" she whispered, and it came from deep within. "I will continue to try!" She sighed. "But if it doesn't work... what can I do? ... What can *I* do alone?"

She took a deep breath, made herself comfortable in the strange bed, and soon fell asleep.

CHAPTER 3: 1993

The Plainfield, New Jersey, Story

A DAWNING OF REALITY

Plainfield is a delightful fusing of past and present. Six beautiful historic districts invite you to explore tree-lined streets and view unique, historic architecture. Best known for its fine Victorian residences, Plainfield is also home to 17th Century and Colonial Revival buildings. Always a cultural center, the city has the oldest community symphony orchestra in the state, the Plainfield Symphony. The Plainfield Arts Festival and the October Festival from the Arts attract visitors from far and wide as does the famous Fourth of July parade. Welcome to Plainfield.

I had arrived just in time for the Eastern Parkway parade: Labor Day in Brooklyn! It was the time when food sellers made a killing, and my aunt's restaurant would not be exempted from this windfall. There was much to prepare for this opportune occasion and so I began working the day I arrived.

One thing that sells well on the parade route is the roti, a very flaky-layered kind of baked dough that easily enfolds curried meats. Between the time I arrived in Plainfield and the dawn of that morning of the parade in New York, I made over six hundred of them. The euphoria of being in America was a monumental motivator. I started work in my aunt's kitchen and continued without a memorable break until very early the next morning. After a short rest and breakfast, I picked up where I had left off —making more rotis deep into the new night and into the new morning. I felt tireless —driven by what I knew was a deep gratitude for what Aunt Claudette was doing for me. She had been the aunt who sent beautiful things from America for me and promised that in time, she would have sent for me to be with her in America... and here I was in Plainfield, New Jersey making all the goodies my grandma and mom taught me to cook. And how much was I going to be paid? It didn't matter to me then; the important thing was: I was in America.

I was given a job in the restaurant my Aunt Claudette and Uncle Gavin owned: *The Turban Restaurant and Catering* on West Front Street in Plainfield, New Jersey. The ambience of *The Turban* will never escape me. African leitmotifs were tastefully distributed about the walls. There were framed prints of elegantly dancing African women; paintings of African Kings and talking drums... paintings of a proud Africa before the advent of the European slave trade. And when my Uncle Gavin chanced to make an appearance on the restaurant's floor, he himself was something to behold in his African robes.

As much as I was proud to be helping my uncle and my aunt, *The Turban* was hardly my Mecca. It only held the genesis of my hopes and fears for my future. Plainfield and *The Turban* for me was the raw reality of having to start over literally from the bottom.

. . .

BASCOM: Can you recall anything while working or living with your aunt and uncle that really brought home the pains of having to start all over?

SHAUN: One day when I was working in my aunt's restaurant—you know—serving strangers... and my little cousin comes up and shouts in the open restaurant —"Cousin Shaun! Cousin Shaun those are *not* your clothes! Why are you wearing *my* auntie's old clothes? (*Chuckles.*) And this is ironic —because I *had* new clothes. My aunt had bought me a couple new things...

BASCOM: (*Nods.*) It was just that on *that* day you happened to be wearing something she gave you from her wardrobe...

SHAUN: Exactly... —I chose to wear the clothes she gave me to work.

BASCOM: So how did you feel when your little cousin blurted out something like that in front of the people you were serving?

SHAUN: How do you think I felt? —How would *you* feel? (*Shakes her head. Slight smile on her face.*) The floor could have opened up and took me! As we said back in Guyana: 'I felt like a cent ice in a desert!' ... I was so humiliated; I hurried through serving the two customers, went to the bathroom, locked the door, and burst into tears.

BASCOM: That was tough...

SHAUN: I had left a great job back in Guyana as loans rep *in a bank!* ... And here I was —a waitress, stroke cook, being humiliated by a child... (*Shakes her head and then chuckles.*) To me it was devastating... I felt so... —

BASCOM: How old was your cousin?

SHAUN: Oh! She was just around five years old, and she had just come in from the day-care...

BASCOM: But continue. —You're in the bathroom...

SHAUN: Yes... I sat in that bathroom and I whispered: "Don't forsake me, God! Please!" I sat there and remembered a time back in Guyana when things between myself and my parents got so bad, I was left with no other alternative but to move in with my boyfriend and his mother in Best Village. I sat in that bathroom and remembered how things were so difficult for the three of us —how tough the living was. I sat in that bathroom in my uncle's restaurant and I said to myself —I said, "Shaun! You asked God to bring you to America for a better life —for a break. Where are you? You *are* in America! Would God bring you all the way here to suffer? NO! Thank God for small mercies, Shaun! —He would *never* give you more than you could bear!"

BASCOM: You steeled your resolve.

SHAUN: About an hour later I washed my face and faced the customers with a smile. Inside, I was a pillar of faith. The thought of returning home was not an option. I was going to survive! I was going to more than merely survive! I was going to *be!*

. . .

DECEMBER. Though deep in her heart Shaun was grateful for what her aunt and her husband were doing for her, on a subconscious level she felt like a runner being held back on the blocks. She didn't mind helping her aunt and her husband until they were able to replace her at the Turban Restaurant.

She was, however, growing very dissatisfied deep within herself and it hurt —ached. Working at the restaurant wasn't easy; being there until after midnight was not uncommon.

She found herself thinking of the cleaner at the library back in Georgetown, Guyana. It was so easy to look down on Miss B; it was easy to pity her ambling along the aisles of books... as she picked up and emptied trash baskets; as she cleaned the library's toilets with a cheerful twinkle in her eyes with crows feet at its corners... as she boasted of her son whom was the head of something or other... as she sat tiredly between the drudgery. Shaun thought of the Miss B, the cleaner... thought of Franz Kafka's *Metamorphosis*... imagined that she was slowly turning into a charwoman, and shuddered. "No way!" Shaun hissed to herself. She had to change this course in her life.

As it was, however, her life was in the hands of her aunt and uncle and that was unacceptable. There was only one way to change things! She had to stand up and take control of the reins of her own life! The thing that also compounded Shaun's predicament in Plainfield was the fact that she had made pledges of remittances to those she cared for back in economically challenged Guyana. But with the money she was making while living and working with her aunt, how *could* she keep them? She had promised her boyfriend and his mother that she would have sent home a barrel for them as early as she could, and had kept it: she scraped together enough money and had mailed home a small Christmas barrel. She did it with love because she knew how bad things were with Carlton and his mom whom had been so good to her.

But doing things like that didn't sit too well with her aunt. Her Aunt Claudette's displeasure left Shaun with a strange feeling. The last thing she wanted to do was upset someone who was so dear to her. She hurt so badly inside of herself she wished she could have been somewhere else. She sensed the beginning of something unpleasant coming between her and her aunt, and it filled her with trepidation. *What should I do? If she tells me to leave where can I go?*

It really wasn't turning out the way Shaun had originally expected. The hours at the restaurant were long and tiring. The euphoria of being in America —working in America was dead.

And so she called her Uncle David—her dad's brother, who lived in Rahway, New Jersey—and detailed her situation to him. He listened and then subtly suggested that she left Plainfield and come stay with him. She grew silent.

"Shaun?"

"I'm here, Uncle David..."

"I *know* you have to think about it, so do that... and get back to me, okay?"

"I definitely will, Uncle David..."

· · ·

I thought of how nomadic my life had been. As long as I could have remembered my life had been a series of moving from one place to another. When I was two years old my paternal grandparents offered to help my very young parents to take care of me, so they took me to live with them at Phoenix Park village on the East Bank of Demerara. I lived with them until I was ten. At that age my father determined I was old enough to help my mom with housework. So my father stopped by my grandparents' house and started a quarrel with his mother. He thought it was high time I returned home. "The plan was not for you to keep my daughter here forever! —Damn it!" The vacation was over. I was then packed against my will and taken back to my parent's home in New Road village. I showed my displeasure of being taken away from my loving grandparents, however, by repeatedly returning to their home to sleep. However, but by the time I passed the Common Entrance Examination and began attending West Demerara Secondary School, I was entrenched in my parents' home, and it was then that I met Carlton Stephenson.

I was just thirteen and my parents didn't take much to him — especially my dad. I guess they were afraid for me —afraid for my obvious gullibility. But in my mind Carlton and I were Christians, and my parents had nothing to fear. I taught Sunday school and Carlton played the guitar in church. I sang solos and he accompanied me. We did many other religious activities together. He was really a good friend who taught me many things.

As we grew towards our mid teens we were content with holding hands. We held ourselves back from having sex because we believed fervently that fornication was a sin against God. We obeyed. But as our hormones began to have the better of us, things changed and we began to take risks.

At age nineteen the relationship between me and my dad fell apart. I packed my things, caught a car to the ferry, went over to my great aunt who lived in a suburb of Georgetown City, and she took me in without a fuss.

I was working at the National Library, but the joy of living in the City was destined not to last. My mother was missing me a lot; my great aunt probably felt guilty about harboring me, and began nagging at me to return home to my parent's house. I told her that I would do as she begged, though I had no intention to.

On the last day of 1989, I called Carlton on the telephone and told him that I was presently leaving my great aunt's home, and had no place to go...

"Can't you go back to your parents place?" he asked.

"Yes, I can, but I'm *not* going back there..."

"So... where are you going to go?"

"Can I live at you... —live with you and your mother?"

He was silent for a while, then he said, "Okay... —why not?"

I crossed back to Vreed-en-hoop and when I saw Carlton waiting there, he did not recognize me. I had lost so much weight due to the heavy stress I had been under. He hugged me and told me not to worry, that I was going to be okay.

"What about your mother?" I asked. "Would it be okay with her —with me staying with you and her?"

He laughed. "When I was asking her if you could, she told me it was my house; that it was up to me —that she has no problem with you living with us..."

I breathed a sight of relief.

"She likes you, Babes," Carlton said.

I sensed, though, that he was uneasy about something. "What is it, Doods?" I asked.

He laughed shyly.

"What?"

"It's not going to be easy living with me and my mom... the house is not very comfortable... and we... —we don't have much to offer as far as the amenities you're used to..."

I assured him that I would be fine.

CHAPTER 4: 2007

Oklahoma

PAINFUL RECOLLECTIONS

Pre-Paid Legal Services Independent Associate Shaun Stephenson, sipped from a glass of iced tea served to her by the Latino waiter in the lounge section of the Best Western hotel. Another informative day at the convention was behind her. The day had been a training day mostly.

But as she sat, she found herself, once again, recalling the Black and Gold Banquet she had been so fortunate to attend. What Shaun found persistently memorable about the experience, was one speaker: Jim Stovall —who had been introduced as a National Olympic weightlifter, Emmy-Award Winner, and world-renowned author.

Like a colossus in a dark suit—and still looking like the champion weightlifter he once was—Jim Stovall came onto the stage and began speaking with rhetorical boldness.

The associate to her left, leaned over and said, "You know that guy's blind?"

"Blind?" Shaun was incredulous. "*He* is blind?"

"Yes," the woman with the African wrap on the right of her said. "Jim Stovall *is* blind. Look carefully at his eyes you'll see..."

Shaun sat there thinking, *Where is his white cane? Where is his seeing-eye dog?* She felt floored even though she was seated. Here was a blind man confidently moving —gesticulating —commanding her attention... —apparently everyone's attention.

She sat there and listened to this man's story of being blind at age twenty-nine... and what he had gone through... and how he got back on track by a little boy who inspired him...

She sipped her ice tea, and in her mind she thought, *WOW! So what excuses do 'I' have not to make it?*

The group of associates with whom she had chitchatted in the lounge earlier, was disappearing into two elevators off to her left. She yawned. Afterwards she heard a hissing sound from some street in the hotel's vicinity. For some reason she could not place, she thought of the sound of the surf on the muddy shores of the Atlantic Ocean where the crabs lurked and four-eye fish wallowed in the shallows... She found herself thinking about husband Carlton —of how he took care of her when she committed herself to that most difficult life with him back on Best Road. She sipped her iced tea and remembered when she was three months pregnant—though neither of them knew it—and had been in a fight with him over some little domestic nonsense that climaxed with her running hysterically into the backyard with him in hot pursuit. She threw herself onto the grass and began threshing about. He tried to calm her, but she would not be consoled. She was tired of their hardships. She stomped and threshed on the hard ground...

Was it then that she lost the child, or was it that *other* day when she jumped that gutter in the process of watering the plants? It was probably then, because soon after, she felt something like a tug —a pull in her belly. That night she experienced a strange feeling in her tummy, followed by agonizing pain that kept her awake. It persisted into the morning, and Carlton's mother took her to see the local gynecologist who did an examination and told her that the fetus was dead.

. . .

Shaun Stephenson thought of her life... her journey. She had left her great aunt's house in the City under the pretext of returning to her parent's home in Crane Village but instead, went by her boyfriend's. Her mother knew that she had left the great aunt's place that day, but was perturbed that Shaun never showed up and night had fallen. Where was she?

The revelation of where Shaun was turned out to be quite dramatic. On the very night of her having settled in with her boyfriend, Carlton's mom met Shaun's mother on the way to church and asked how she was doing.

"What I will tell you girl?" Shaun's mother said. "You make children and sometimes you make problems!"

"What happen, Jean, girl?"

"Shaundal," Shaun's mother began, shaking her head. "Shaundal move out my house, and start living with she great aunt in 'Town; well just today the aunt tell me Shaun left to come back to my house —but up to now me or the father ain't seen her! It soon going be twelve midnight and nobody ain't know where Shaun is —nobody!"

"Don't worry, Jean. Shaun at me..."

For a moment Jean Harry was speechless, then: "WHAT YOU TELLING ME, JOYCE? —*MY* DAUGHTER AT YOU? —WITH *YOU* SON? —IN *YOU* HOUSE?"

Jean began cursing Joyce who shrugged it off.

"I don't care what you say! Shaun and Carlton is adults! —I not asking Shaun to leave —and I not asking my son go!"

Shaun mom's confronted her. "I want you to leave these people house now-now, girl!"

But Shaun stood her ground as her own woman and refused. It was her life; *she* was going to make decisions for herself.

In the end her mother, bitter and distraught, left Shaun to her fate.

She sipped her iced tea and thought of her mom who now lived with her in Mantua, New Jersey, and smiled deep within her psyche.

CHAPTER 5: 2007

Oklahoma

CONVENTION-AL VALUES

Shaun sat at the little table in the hotel's lounge and looked at her wristwatch. There were a few calls still to be made before she considered her working day over. Physically, she was tired; emotionally, however, she felt pumped —on the threshold of great opportunities.

The session that day was especially exciting in the light of the new threshold Pre-Paid Legal Services was stepping over. With identity theft sweeping the country as one of the fastest growing crimes, Pre-Paid Legal had positioned itself to help anyone protect against this scourge. There were training sessions that day to help Independent Associates understand their role in educating the public about ID theft, and how Pre-Paid Legal Services was positioned to help.

Shaun had learnt much about how she could elevate herself in the Pre-Paid Legal business. She was also very excited about the new information she would be able to share with her South-Jersey team members who had not made it to Oklahoma City. The sign-up fee, for example, for anyone wanting to become an Independent Associate with Pre-Paid Legal Services Incorporated (PPLSI), was going to remain at forty-nine dollars. There was also a special sign-up fee of twenty-five dollars for individuals who were single; this was new.

"Don't forget, Shaun!" reminded an associate passing by. "Executive Director David Allen needs to have a very brief meeting with us, okay?"

"I won't," she quips and laughs.

"And how have you been, Shaun?" another associate asked, his wife's arm hooked into his.

"Quite extraordinary, you know," Shaun said.

"Extraordinary! I like that..." Then he added, laughing, "I see you were quite hyped up listening to Dave Savula's speech..."

"And so were you, Jim!"

"Weren't we all..." he said laughing.

"Goodnight, Shaun," his wife said. "See you at tomorrow's session!"

"You two have a good night also."

Her cell phone began a rhythm almost Caribbean. "Shaun," she answered pleasantly and laughed as the Oklahoma night wound up to midnight and destined for a new day.

"Maryetta..."

"Hi, Maryetta... —retiring now?"

Maryetta Marks was a fellow Pre-Paid Legal Independent associate and they had become good friends. Maryetta Marks, who was also a Defense Attorney out of California, was more than an associate to Shaun; at times she acted as though Shaun was a younger sister. Maryetta was in her fifties and looked great.

Shaun wished Maryetta had been staying at the Best Western also. Instead she was staying over at the Renaissance some fifteen minutes away by the shuttle service. And once more Shaun was thinking of the Black and Gold Banquet. After she and Zonia had returned from it, she did not head back to the Best Western where her mom and aunt were. She had stayed over in Maryetta's room at the Renaissance that was close to the Convention Hall where the Banquet had been held.

"So what are you doing, Maryetta?"

"Turning in to bed," Maryetta said, yawning covertly over the phone. "I just said to myself: let me give Shaun a goodnight shout..."

"Okay, then," Shaun chortled. "Have a good night, then, Maryetta —see you tomorrow..."

"Night-night, Shaun..."

Shaun closed her phone and thought of her husband. *Maybe when I get back things will change... my business will pick up, and things will be better between us...*

She discarded the Styrofoam cup into a recyclable bin and rose to her feet.

CHAPTER 6: 1993

The Plainfield Story Continues

PAINFUL TRANSITIONS

I guess my Aunt Claudette and her husband somehow saw me as a catalyst of good things happening for them in the competitive business of being restaurateurs. I guess they both saw me as an integral key in things turning *The Turban* into more profitable winds. I knew I was being a great help to their endeavor. But I had had enough of restaurant work and told my aunt that I was going to leave for Rahway, and my Uncle David. It didn't sit well with her, and that I understood.

Things became very awkward between us for a while. One morning when it was snowing heavily she drove to the restaurant without me. *The Turban* was a mile or so away. I had to walk through the snow and the going was rough — tenuous: I slipped many times... fell a couple of times. I discovered that the white stuff that once looked so homely and beautiful in the Christmas cards we received from overseas wasn't so nice.

I knew my Aunt Claudette was hurting, but I too had an American dream though I didn't know exactly what it was. I had left my job as a respected loans representative back in Guyana and came with great aspirations to the United States; I had come to America for a better life and being a waitress in *The Turban* was not it.

· · ·

BASCOM: There you were on the verge of moving to your Uncle David's —starting another chapter in America. Were you scared?

SHAUN: I was *never* scared of anything!

BASCOM: Tell me about the actual move from Plainfield. Was there any drama?

SHAUN: Not really you know... My Uncle David came by my aunt's house to pick me up around the midday on that New Year's Eve. She was at the restaurant. I wasn't working anymore because my move had been impending for the last few days. I was already packed and had been waiting for my uncle to pick me up. (*Shrugs.*) So he came; I said goodbye to my cousin —Gavin, and left for Rahway... It was a long drive... That night Uncle David's mother-in-law had a house party and they took me.

BASCOM: You *would* say it was a neat transition...

SHAUN: It was.

CHAPTER 7: 1994

The Rahway, New Jersey, Story

Since World War II, Rahway, like many municipalities in the Northeast, lost much of its industrial base as factory jobs shifted south or overseas. The city has seen the rise of service-dependent jobs within its borders and growth in finance, pharmaceuticals and telecommunications throughout the region as Rahway residents traveled throughout New Jersey and New York for employment. Now beginning the 21st Century, Rahway is a diverse middle-class community of 26,500 that has been reinventing itself in the post-industrial age and will be celebrating 150 years of its incorporation as a city in 2008.

JANUARY. I was still experiencing lingering anxiety mixed with traces of guilt for leaving Plainfield and my Aunt Claudette, but I had to think about myself. The grass, however, was not greener in Rahway with Uncle David and his little family that comprised of Sharon, his wife, Zanette, their teenage daughter, and Brandon who had just turned one year old.

My Uncle David and his wife Sharon were more laid back. They saw me as someone who would help out until I found a job. Before I came, Sharon, my uncle, and Zanette—who went to Rahway High—shared the baby-sitting: Aunt Sharon took care of Brandon during the night because she was a nurse and her day shift enabled her to. My uncle looked at Brandon during the day because he was a night-shift assembly line supervisor with General Motors, and Zanette helped after she came home from school. With me there, it was added assistance with taking care of Brandon.

I felt so much at home with my uncle and his family in that very first week, and quickly grew to love my cousins. Brandon was a lovable handful who liked to play with my hair and lie on my stomach. It was soul soothing to smell his baby smell and to drink in his baby smile and giggles of pure innocence. Zanette was a very pretty, pleasant fourteen-year-old who, I guessed, took an immediate liking to me. She seemed an excitable girl at heart with an eye for fashion. She liked to do variations on my braided hair... sometimes beads... sometimes she would plait it into threes... sometimes in a bun. During that first week at my Uncle David's she was good company when she came home from high school. She helped me take care of Brandon and showed me around Rahway.

But I was determined not to be at my uncle's home for very long. I needed to find a job as quickly as possible, and spoke to my Aunt Sharon about it. She was very supportive. She told me not to despair, that I was young —that there were immense opportunities for someone of my age and with my background. I always remembered her for that. She encouraged me to check the classifieds in the *Star Ledger* that was tossed onto the front porch daily.

· · ·

As Brandon slept, Shaun stood at a window of her Uncle David's Rahway home. She looked out beyond the pines that towered aback the houses over Essex Street and knew she would not be helping with baby-sitting until the end of the month. She *was* going to find a job.

The next morning Zanette brought her *The Star Ledger* once again, and she started going through the classified pages. There was an ad placed by a gentleman, one Mr. M who was looking for a seven-day live-in housekeeper. He was going to pay one hundred and seventy-five dollars a week. That evening when her Aunt Sharon came home, Shaun said to her, "I think I saw a live-in job in the newspapers that I won't mind applying for..."

"Good for you, Shaun! —Call the number and see if you can secure an interview, and I'm sure David will gladly take you... —where is it?"

"Some place named Tom's River..."

"Your uncle can take you. Make the call."

Shaun made the call; an interview appointment was set, and her uncle drove her to Toms River where she met one Mr. M. He was a Jewish gentleman with thinning hair and a balding pate. He greeted them with a smile that lacked practice and invited them in. It was an airy house with a welcoming atmosphere, but there was something about seventy-something-year-old Mr. M that turned Shaun off. He wore jeans and a leather jacket and on his feet were the popularized Timberlands. To her, he looked like an old man who didn't want to be old. Somehow that didn't sit well with her. In her mind, such old men, tended to be fresh.

Mr. M invited them to sit and soon they were past the obligatory *where are you from* and *are you eligible to work yada, yada...* Mr. M detailed what the duties were, should she accept the job —general cleaning, bland-food cooking: not-too-much-oil-not too much-spices...

"How would I be paid?" Shaun asked.

"What do you mean 'how'?" Mr. M said with a slight trace of irritation. "We decided that it would be cash, didn't we?"

"I mean will it be weekly?" she said.

"I always pay on the last day of the month," he said. "The way the Africans were paid." he said.

The way the Africans were paid! Shaun was taken aback. *Does he mean slaves?*

"Are you going to take the job, Shaun?" Uncle David asked.

She nodded. "I'll take it," she said and looked into her uncle's eyes; he looked into hers and his eyes asked: *Are you sure about this, Shaun?*

But she was elated about finally finding a job paying more than she expected.

"I'm going to take it," she said.

The old man smiled. "The job's yours... Let me give you a tour of my home..." he said and rose to his feet. He was about five, nine.

He chipped ahead of her. It was a ranch-styled house on two levels: the first floor and the basement —three bedrooms, one bath, an eat-in kitchen and a living room with a television and an exercise bike.

. . .

Driving back to Rahway, they were both silent for a stretch until her uncle said, "He pays at the end of the month! —What these people think at all?" He shook his head as she gazed out the window. "He pays like how the Africans were paid! —Shaun, do you realize what that guy meant?"

"I was wondering about that too... I only hope he didn't mean that he pays the way his kind once paid slaves."

Her uncle David shook his head angrily. She understood his anger; but her mind was made up. She was going to do whatever it took to make it —to help her family back in Guyana. There was no turning back no matter how treacherous the road ahead looked. The car hummed along. It was a Friday and Shaun was destined to start her first real job in Toms River, New Jersey, the following Monday.

CHAPTER 8: 1994

The Tom's River, New Jersey, Story

FENDING OFF SEXUAL MOLESTATION

The Township of Toms River is a township in Ocean County, New Jersey, and the county seat of Ocean County. In 2006, Toms River was ranked by Morgan Quitno as the fourteenth safest "city" in the United States, of 369 cities nationwide.

JANUARY. I accompanied Mr. M in his tired Ford Bronco truck to the supermarket and discovered the true meaning of frugality. He gravitated towards the food-sample offerings on display about the store. I guessed he reasoned that if filled himself with sample bites here and toothpicked bits there, there would be no reason to have to cook after our shopping excursion. When it came to the actual shopping, Mr. M bought the cheapest of everything. His list often carried one head of broccoli, two apples, five bananas —calculated to last five days, five lemons —calculated to last five mornings, one small pack of chicken breast —calculated to last one week... In short whatever went into our cart was limited to one of each item on his wretched shopping list.

I began cooking for him and was introduced to an entirely new way of preparing meals. He used no salt; he used no sugar, and was very particular about how I prepared his meals. Breakfast would be fresh ground coffee, bean-brewed. I was required to have a glass of warm water into which one lemon was squeezed. A few pieces of fruit or fresh-squeezed fruit juice completed his morning meal. Mr. M's lunch was normally one piece of chicken breast or one piece of fish along with a glass of fruit juice. Dinner was fresh salad with either a bit of fish or chicken with a spoon of fresh-ground peanut butter or one scoop of ice cream.

I reluctantly ate what I cooked for him and began losing weight. I hadn't money of my own to purchase my kind of groceries and cook the meals I had been accustomed to. The thought of using his groceries to cook for myself was out of the question. He checked his food supply day to day with almost military regularity. Things were earmarked to last until it was time to visit the supermarket each successive Friday.

I began to regret taking the job even before the month was over. What I was required to do was worth times the amount of money I was destined to receive. Bitterness began to seep into me and I thought of my Aunt Claudette... my Uncle Gavin... my Uncle David and his wife Sharon. I knew I had made a big mistake, but I also knew that it would be through my mistakes that I would become the woman I was going to be —that through the lessons from my mistakes I would one day rise beyond all setbacks. I steeled my resolve and did what I had to do in M's 'plantation.' My duties included all chores in the house. I once found myself with a paint roller in my hands.

My very first experience of a blizzard was in Tom's River. The garbage had to be taken out to the curb. I stepped into the yard and sank almost hip-deep in the snow and began wading —stumbling my way to the sidewalk.

Things took a turn for the worse one night when there was snowstorm. I could have heard the wind howling through the trees and the thumping of the branches against my bedroom window. Through it I was sure that I heard Mr. M in the living room and got up from my bed and closed the door. He told me that the bedroom door should always be wide open at nights to allow air to pass through the house freely. That, however, made me uneasy about my privacy. The storm raged on and maybe I got used to it and dozed off. Around midnight I stirred and awoke in alarm. There was someone sneaking under my covers. I jumped out of bed, rushed to the night table and switched on the lamp. Mr. M was in my bed. My body shuddered at the look on his red, wrinkled, grinning face.

"HOW DARE YOU?" I demanded —my lips trembling. "WHAT THE HELL ARE YOU DOING IN MY BED? —YOU CANNOT DO THIS! —HOW DARE YOU DISRESPECT ME LIKE THIS? —YOU CANNOT DO THIS! —PLEASE LEAVE OR *I* WILL LEAVE!"

He was taken aback by my outburst. "Please... please!" he pleaded as he stood in his pajamas. "Please... I was cold... —a-and I was hoping we can lie together and warm each other..."

I stormed out of the room, and he left for his. Below my indignation, however, I was shaken —afraid. *Oh my God, what is this?* I spent the rest of the night in an easy chair in the living room but could not sleep.

The next morning he apologized profusely.

"Mr. M, I work for you! —But what *you* did last night does *not* figure into *any* of the duties you assigned!"

"I'm truly sorry —I really am. Again forgive me... —please!"

"All I have to tell you is: just stay away from me —and respect yourself!"

Did he?

It was my duty, after his breakfast was ready, to rap on his door and wake him up each day. One morning he asked me to enter, and when I did I could not believe my eyes. Mr. M lay naked in bed.

"My skin," he said, beckoning to me. "Could you please cream my skin?"

My first impulse was to walk out and call my Uncle David to take me back to Rahway. I composed myself and turned my face away from the pathetic sight. "Please, Sir!" I said with all the courage I could have mustered, "I am *not* your nurse!" Then I got angry: "This is so disrespectful, Mr. M! —I CAME HERE AS YOUR HOUSEKEEPER AND WOULD DO *NO* MORE THAN THAT!" And fighting back tears I retreated to the kitchen and began preparing his breakfast in anger, in humiliation, and feeling sick to the pit of my stomach. And my tears, blinding, just came.

What can I do? —Oh God!

I was on a visitor's visa, wasn't supposed to be working, couldn't call the Authorities, and he knew it.

"I'm sorry," he said from behind me.

This time I said nothing. Many things ran through mind. I could not stay her under these impertinent advances, but I needed the money and it was just under one more week before the month was over... *one more week and I can pack my bags and go! But go where? I didn't want to be a burden to anyone—anymore! I can go back to my Uncle David's home, but there was no future there. I would cook and clean and take care of baby Brandon, but I won't be paid. I was being paid here. I'm going to stay!*

Things went well for just a few days and then the worst happened. One morning while I was taking a shower Mr. M abruptly pulled the curtain open and attempted to join me. I grabbed my towel, covered myself and shouted in his face.

"YOU DIRTY OLD SLIME! —HOW DARE YOU DISRE-GARD MY PRIVACY! —THIS IS IT! —ONCE AND FOR ALL! —THIS IS THE LAST TIME YOU'LL EVER HARASS ME! —I AM LEAVING!"

It was just two days before the month ended. My hands trembled as I dressed quickly. I called my uncle. "Please pick me up, Uncle David! —Things aren't working out here!" I'm sure my voice shook.

"What's wrong, Shaun?"

"Please pick me up, Uncle David! —Please!" and I began to cry.

"Okay, Shaun... I'll be there as soon as I can..."

"Thanks, Uncle David..."

Mr. M had left the house for some time before returning to plead and beg forgiveness. I refused to speak to him. He then gave me an envelope with seven hundred dollars, though I did not look to see what was inside of it, then.

At last my uncle arrived to take me back to Rahway, and the saga of Toms River ended.

· · ·

Back at her uncle's, Shaun once more helped with baby Brandon. It took her approximately one week to gather herself together again, and began scoring the classified pages of *The Star Ledger* once again. One morning she came upon a job opening for a nanny to take care of five children in Summit, New Jersey. One Dr. D and his wife, Daisy, had placed the ad. She called the number and secured an interview.

Her Aunt Sharon drove her to the St. Barnabas Hospital in Livingston, New Jersey and Shaun met Doctor D. He looked at her, nodded, and said, "I like your smile... you're hired. —So what's next? Tomorrow I want you to meet my wife and the kids, okay?"

At little after seven the next day, I set out with my uncle along heavy snow-bound streets for an interview with the Doctor's wife. Along the way I prayed that his wife was as accommodating as he was. Somehow I was sure that once I got this job, a defini-tive chapter in my life would soon begin.

At last we swung into the street where the doctor lived, and pulled up to this expansive yard with playing children before a massive four-story colonial. My uncle pulled in close to one of the towering oaks. On the bole the house number was professionally engraved. Way over to the other side of it another oak stood proud. Sentinels. Uncle David cut the engine and I got out. The children who were playing in the snow paused to see who had arrived. Four of them huddled and spoke briefly before resuming their play.

I stepped up to a gigantic front door encompassed by an extended wrap-around porch. I took a deep breath, rang the bell, and waited. Soon enough, I heard footsteps quickly descending a stair. The door opened. A tall, red-haired woman with a pleasant countenance greeted me.

"Hi, you must be Shaun —I'm Daisy, the Doctor's wife —come in..."

I entered. Before me there was a grand, curving staircase that ascended to a second floor. On the left of me was an area before an enormous fireplace, and there was a real fire going —real wood burning. This was amazing. I had only read about such in the classic English novels in which, it seemed someone sat reading before a fireplace. I gazed around. Over from the fireplace area, and on the right of where I stood, was a large living room beyond which an arrangement of sliding panels offered a view of a vast dining room and kitchen. I felt as if I were in a grand castle and I realized the magnitude of the job, should I be hired.

"The interview is going to be very formal, Shaun... let's go to the kitchen..."

When we got there I saw a baby boy in the lower section of a cupboard. He looked at me, smiled, crawled out and grabbed onto my legs. I picked him up and he began playing with my face.

"Oh, Wow! —This is interesting," Daisy said. "He likes you."

"I like him too...—what's his name?"

"Matthew... —we call him Matt..."

"How old is he?"

"Nine months..."

I could have sensed Mrs. D she was really trying to be cheery with me though I could have seen —could have felt how flustered she was. I later learned why: The children's nanny of five years had upped and left.

"Shaun, if you accept the job, I'll be hiring you to take care of

Matthew primarily, you know, along with doing general house-work... laundry —things like that —But taking care of Matt here would be your main duty. As for cooking, you will not be required to cook, okay?"

"Okay..."

"I know you must have looked around and wondered how you were going to take care of things in such a large house..." Daisy smiled. "Don't worry there's a woman who comes in to do general cleaning —scrubbing the bathrooms and changing the sheets —vacuuming —dusting and all that stuff..."

"Okay..."

"Now, this is important: Next week, the doctor and I will be going on a vacation from the kids for one week, and whoever we hire will be responsible for the security of the home and the children..."

She was looking keenly at me now. I was caught off-guard with the vacation bit, but tried not to show it.

"No problem. If I'm given the job I will be able to handle that..."

"Good... I take it, then, that you *are* accepting the job."

"Yes." Baby Matthew was playing with my lips.

"He likes you!" Daisy chortled. "Let's hope the other four does. They are the ones who hire the nanny."

Soon afterwards the others came in... one by one.

Brittany who was three and a half, screamed with glee. "Mommy —Mommy! Is this our new nanny?" She hugged my legs and continued: "Could you please be my nanny? Please? Please?"

Daisy said: "Did the Doctor —my husband tell you how much we propose to pay you?"

"It was in the papers —remember?"

"Oh yes... —but would that be okay with you, Shaun?"

"That's fine with me..."

The other children came into the kitchen. First there was Roger who was seven, Benjamin who was eight, and Thomas the eldest: He was eleven but shy. They all seemed very happy to meet me. They all wanted me to be their new nanny.

"Can you start on Monday, Shaun?"

"Yes... —I can..." I said, feeling little Matthew's warmth, smelling his baby smell.

"Okay!" Daisy said with laughter in her voice.

I was hired. It was a done deal.

CHAPTER 9: 2007

Oklahoma

AFTER THE BLACK AND GOLD BANQUET

Shaun and Zonia entered the large hotel room where Maryetta and the others waited to hear about the Black and Gold Banquet. Every one of the women in the room seemed to be saying, "Tell me!" —"Tell me!! —"Tell me!" at the same time.

"Girls!" Maryetta said laughing. "Let them breathe..." Then she turned back to Shaun and Zonia. "So tell us how it was? —You don't know how I wish I was able to attend the banquet..."

"You were there in spirit, Maryetta," Shaun said. Then to all in the room: "You were all there in spirit with me and Zonia..."

Maryetta chuckled. "Shaun, you sound like a politician."

"I'm sorry," Shaun said laughing.

"So tell us about it —what was the experience like?" Maryetta said. And from the look of excitement in the other women's eyes she spoke for them too.

Shaun turned to Zonia. "You want to go first?"

"No, Shaun —you tell it. You're more articulate..."

"Come' on, Zonia! —You're as articulate as anyone I know!"

"I'd rather you tell it," Zonia, ever modest, insisted.

Shaun looked into the women's faces. Many of them had grown close to her and most of them were much older. This was something that Shaun, thirty-seven years old, marveled about: Most of her business associates were fifteen —twenty years her senior. In her country it might have been said, jocularly, that it was so because Shaun was born old.

"Well girls," Shaun began. "The Black and Gold Banquet was grand! —So where do you want me to start?"

. . .

The opening highlight of the Pre-Paid Legal International Convention in Oklahoma City was its Black and Gold Banquet, and Shaun was hoping she qualified to attend. It was the ceremony of ceremonies for the recognition of the best of the best Directors in the Pre-Paid Legal Service system. She had tried very hard to qualify for attendance, but missed it by a few points. A few days before she had flown off to Oklahoma, however, Shaun received a phone call from Texas. It was from Executive Director David Allen, her Pre-Paid Legal mentor and coach.

"Shaun... have you ever attended the Banquet before?"

"*The* Black and Gold Banquet?"

"The same..."

"No, I haven't ..."

"Well..."

"Well? —Well what, David?"

He laughed. "Well make sure you pack a pretty dress because I have tickets for you and Zonia to attend it..."

"What are you telling me, David? —Oh my Gosh! —IS THIS FOR REAL? —DO YOU REALLY MEAN THAT? —I GET TO ATTEND THE BLACK AND GOLD BANQUET IN OKLAHOMA?"

"Yes, Shaun. For all the hard work you put in —for all of your commitment over the past months... you deserve it..."

Tears welled in her eyes and emotion filled the pits of her stomach.

He continued: "You and Zonia will be attending in my place."

"THANK YOU, DAVID! —Thank you! —Thank you! —Thank you! —Thank you! —You're a blessing!"

She was amazed —stunned. Just a few minutes before the phone rang she had been telling her Aunt Bridget the bad news: that she did not make 'the cut' to attend the Banquet this time. "There's always next time, my niece," her aunt had said. "There's always next time..." Shaun shrugged it off and was inspired work even harder for the next Convention to come. And then David Allen was on the line and everything changed.

"See you in Oklahoma, Shaun," David Allen said.

"Thank you, again, David..."

"You're always welcome, Shaun..."

Right away she called Zonia her business PPLSI partner over in California. Zonia too had heard the great news from David.

The exhilaration was mutual, and it continued to be so after they met in Oklahoma City.

The night before the Convention, Shaun and Zonia got together at the Renaissance Hotel and reminisced about their achievements over the past six months. Women from other teams were also in the room. They all seemed excited that two from *their* level had been elevated to attend the grand function.

Shaun and Zonia spoke about not knowing what to expect; they spoke about how fulfilling the experience may well be: to be in the same room with Pre Paid Legal's top money-earners —maybe even shake hands with a few of them —the very individuals they read about and saw in the Pre Paid Legal magazines and DVDs... She and Zonia anticipated a WOW! experience.

The night of the banquet was memorable! Shaun wore a loose, conservative, black pantsuit. Zonia too was dressed in black. Shaun remembered how it was stepping onto the red carpet that ushered them into the Banquet Hall. She felt like the storybook duckling that morphed into a swan. The atmosphere was beautiful... Music played softly. Arrayed about the vast hall were huge, round tables —each elegantly decorated with magnificent floral arrangements. There was an elevated stage caught between a pair of huge pillars from which were hung fine fabrics in the shades of lilac, eggshell, soft pinks, and yellows. To her this was an occasion for royalty.

· · ·

"It was breathtaking, I tell you! —It was a grand moment when the proceedings started and I began hearing the stories that so many had gone through to stand successful on that stage. And as the honorees spoke, it was as if each spoke directly to me —saying to me: 'Shaun, do not quit! —Stick with it! Stay with it, Shaun! And it will be worth it!' ... There was this girl in a wheel chair that told her story... She had two children and lived out of her car... They took showers in places like gyms, she said. And there she was standing on that stage —a successful Pre-Paid Legal Associate..."

"You're giving me goose pimples, girlfriend..."

"And when Jim Stovall —a blind man! —The author of 'The

Ultimate Gift' told his story... —It was incredible! What excuses have we not to succeed with what we know in our hearts that we can do?

"I sat there and tears filled my eyes..."

"Wow..."

"It was an experience and I wish you all were there! —I will remember that Black and Gold Banquet for the rest of my life— you know —sitting among ordinary people who have accomplished extraordinary things... and I was able to sit... and listen... and connect... and learn from the best."

. . .

Later that night in Maryetta's room at the Renaissance Hotel, Shaun thought of David Allen... father-figure David Allen whom had guided her to what she now was, a Director within the Pre-Paid Legal Services Inc. structure. She smiled to remember the State Chamber networking event that she and David had gone to, and how she became overwhelmed and approached David in a panic and whispered urgently to him, "David! We got to go! —I can't do this! —We've got to go! Now!" And even though it had happened so long ago, he would still tell about it. But it was David who pushed her into leadership roles and began encouraging, teaching, and training her in mentoring new Pre-Paid Legal Services Independent Associates.

She sighed and lay back in bed. *God bless the Davids of this world.*

She glanced over to Maryetta and Garletta snoring lightly in rounds. Shaun's thoughts, though, were of her husband. In a few days she would be flying home to him.

CHAPTER 10: 1994

The Summit, New Jersey, Story

DISCOVERING NEW STRENGTH: THE BIRTHING OF A LIVE-IN NANNY AND MAID

Originally, Summit was a cozy farming community populated by about 300 people until 1837. The community began to change from a rural farming and milling to quasi-commercial. After the Civil War, Summit became a summer resort area because of its crisp, clean mountain air and convenient proximity to New York City. Summit attracted extremely wealthy people who built extensive summer estates. Summit is a family-oriented residential community with light industry.

It was nippy-cold that February morning when I arrived at the D's Mansion to start my first day of work with the family. I looked at myself in a hallway mirror with an ornate frame... a heavily braided young woman looked back at me. In the eyes was a yearning to understand her present and a desperate prayer for a hope-filled future. I looked at the face and tried to be brave —tried not to regret —tried not to remember myself sitting at my loans-rep. desk prioritizing applications... tried not to remember myself being photographed by Tyrone in the shade of a flamboyant tree...

Footsteps.

I turned away from the mirror. The Doctor's wife, Daisy, was returning.

"Well-well..." she said with a practiced smile. "We're here."

I smiled. "We're here..."

What in God's name am I doing here? I thought as Daisy began giving me a tour of the house. *How will I take care of five children? What do I know about childcare really? Yes, being the eldest grandchild, I took care of my younger cousins back in Guyana, but these are White children! —American children! And in one week's time this woman and her husband will be away on vacation and they'll be leaving me in charge of their children and this—this huge mansion... Have I bitten off more than I can chew? But what alternative do I have? Go back to The Turban? Go back home to Guyana?*

Neither was an option; my mind was made up.

I can do this job!

And as I trailed behind Daisy D, I told myself that I would do my new job well, but in my heart I silently prayed: *Lord give me the understanding to pull this off! —Help me! —Give me the strength!*

"Okay, Shaun... first things first... the kitchen..."

On the way there, I passed what seemed a closet for coats and toys. Out of it clothes were heaped in disorder. There was a line of dropped clothing that led off to another stair that led down to a basement. There was more clothing on the floor that led to the kitchen that I after Daisy. I was confronted with unwashed dishes that filled the sink —dirty dishes on the running boards and cupboard tops... dishes encrusted with food from the weekend still on the table...

"Okay, Shaun," Daisy said. "Now let me give you the grand tour..."

"Okay..."

"As we're on this level, Shaun, we're going to start from the basement?"

"Why not?"

With little Matt in my arms, I followed Daisy into the basement. It was yet another expansive living area that was furnished. What concerned me, however, was the vast amount of children's clothing scattered and piled in the area where the mammoth washer and dryer stood. Right away I knew that doing the laundry would be my hardest chore. In that basement too, was the baby's playpen. It was where he was destined to be while I was doing housework.

In the basement also, there was a large pantry that affected me in a strange way. There was so much food... food that I had never seen before. There were all kinds of groceries —canned, boxed, and bottled... —everything —from peas and beans and oil... —I felt as though I had wandered into a little grocery store. It affected me because back in my country it was unusual to stock that amount of food at home... and as I looked at that I said in my mind, *Wow! These people have food to last maybe a year of more...*

"Okay, Shaun... now we'll go to the second floor..."

On the second floor, there were four bedrooms that included the self-contained master bedroom. Then there was another that belonged to Brittany, and another that belonged to the two bigger boys. Even baby Matt had his own sleeping space. There were two bathrooms on that floor. Beyond Matt's space, there was vast all-season sunroom with audio and video entertainment systems. Each room was a portrait of chaos. There were beds to be made, bathrooms to be cleaned, closets of clothes to be sorted. I wondered what I had gotten myself into, and one thought was dominant in my mind: *Where do I begin to clean up this mess?*

And as if Daisy had read my mind, she said, "I know it looks overwhelming, but it only *looks* that way; I'm going to help you get going."

"Okay..."

"Now, let me take you to the third floor..."

On the third floor was the big boy's space, and yet another bathroom.

"Now... let me show you your room, Shaun..."

I followed Daisy into the maid's room and stepped onto a fluffy carpet. The walls were beautifully papered. There was a twin bed with pretty pillows in cases with floral designs. There was a neat, little vanity with a matching chair. There was also a walk-in closet. Right above the bed there were wide windows with pink, frilly, striped curtains. Once I got out of bed the windows would be right there. I could actually step off the bed and be right there by the windows. There was also a TV and a telephone. It looked like a Princess's room.

"This is your space, Shaun," Daisy said. "Feel free to do whatever it is you want up here..."

"Thank you, Daisy..."

"So what you can do today is bring up your stuff and settle in..."

I didn't have much stuff... just a little duffle bag with some simple toiletries, and two to three pieces of clothing —a couple jeans and a few shirts. When I began to work, I interchanged a pair of outfits.

"Relax a while, Shaun," Daily was saying. "Later I'll come, get you, and help you get started —wherever you choose to start. Okay?"

"Okay..."

Then she left, taking the baby with her.

That she gave me the option to start with whatever chores I fancied, struck me as kind of unusual. *Where was the list?* I had been told that, most likely, there was going to be a list on the fridge or somewhere, coldly detailing my duties. Daisy, however, just left the order of chores open to me. The outlook didn't look too bad.

So there I was alone in my room. And as I sat on the bed gazing out the window, I couldn't help but feel a kind of relief. Here was a family that did not know me, but took to me on face value. Here was a family that took me in. I was going to be living with them and going back to my Uncle's place only on weekends.

From the windows I could have seen parts of the building's exterior. The size of it amazed me. I felt so proud to be part of something so grand —so humungous! I knew that there were so many things I needed to learn about life in America. I knew I needed guidance, and felt that this was the place where I was going to get it! I was ecstatic to have landed a job with this affluent family. Through the D's I was going to learn the culture of this impressive country.

I looked out to a wintry landscape and felt my American dream unfolding. I stood there and felt as if it were my very first day in America.

· · ·

BASCOM: Can you give me *one* day of your life as a nanny with the D family? In a chronological order, I mean — from the time you get up from your bed to the time you climb back into your bed.

SHAUN: Okay... I get out of bed at say... six in the morning... head to the shower and get myself clean and ready for the day... Then I head down to Matthew's room. Most times I would find him playing in his crib, or he might be as miserable as any wet baby can be. I would take him out of those clothes and give him a bath in the tub with his floaters —his rubber ducks and toys like that... then I would put on his first change of clothes for the day...

After that, I would take him on my hip and make the rounds to wake up the other children. First Brittany, then Benjamin and Roger. Thomas the eldest, who slept on my floor, woke himself.

By now it is about 7:15 A.M. and I'm heading down to the kitchen to deposit Matt in his high chair and get him a bottle of formula. I would get breakfast for his brothers and sister. Breakfast was what ever *they* wanted. It could have been waffles and milk or hot chocolate or orange juice. It could have been cereal or cereal and milk...

By 8: 00 A.M. they're finished breakfast and getting their school stuff organized... —By Now Daisy is down and urging them to be ready since she has to take them to school in the Volvo wagon...

By 8:30: AM everyone has left the house and it is Matt and myself to face the rest of the day until they return.

At this point, I get myself some breakfast. I would take two slices of toast, a few slices of cheese, or a peanut butter and jelly sandwich with a cup of tea... After eating something I would start getting dishes together and into the dishwasher... clean the tables... clean the counters...

BASCOM: At this point, where is the baby?

SHAUN: Matt is in his high chair after I would have fed him something Gerber.

After the dishes and the surfaces, I would clean the floor —sweep or mop —most times mop because the kids being kids drop food on the floor.

By 9:00 — 9:30 AM. I'm back in Matt's room on the second floor, to clean his crib and replace the bedding. Afterwards I would put him back into his crib and leave him there a while. I would then head to the bedrooms... (*Shakes her head.*) The bedrooms... I would always start with the Master bedroom. There, I would take the used beddings off, make a pile of dirty sheets and stuff on the floor, and then I would make up the bed... I would then move to the children's' bedrooms which—you'd imagine—would be strewn with dropped clothing and toys and footwear... (*Shrugs.*) What I did in the master bedroom, would be the same things I would do in the children's rooms —make the beds, clean up, and put all the dirty stuff in piles... Later I would retrieve the pile of dirty clothes from the master bedroom, and the dirty piles of clothing from the children's rooms and lug them to the laundry room in the basement.

BASCOM: What about the bathrooms?

SHAUN: The bathrooms were a special challenge for me. The biggest to clean was the master bathroom that adjoined the boys' bedroom. Cleaning that bathroom began with me picking up towels from the floor... taking down whatever is hanging on the bathroom door... clean the mirrors —sink and the toilet bowl... —I would repeat this process three times...

BASCOM: Three bathrooms...

SHAUN: (*Nods.*) By now it's close to 11:00 AM.

BASCOM: So what time did you get about doing that massive amount of laundry?

SHAUN: What I would do is this: Between doing the bathrooms I would be taking loads of towels and other such stuff down to the basement in order to get a head start up on the laundry. In a way, I did the bathrooms and laundry sort of simultaneously. By now it's lunchtime. I would feed Mat and grab myself a tuna fish sandwich or a cheese sandwich. After that, I would take him to his playpen in the basement. Let me tell you some more about the basement area. It was vast. It was where the children played. There was a huge sectional before a TV, and there were clothes and toys everywhere. In a corner was a workstation with a computer that Daisy sometimes used when she was working at home. There was also a pantry and a half bath. Other than doing the laundry, I would have to clean the entire basement. The children always had it in a mess. Because most of the visitors to the D's home came through the basement where all the kids and their friends hung out, it was important that the basement be kept clean.

BASCOM: What time is it now?

SHAUN: By now it is close to 2:00 PM. And Matt is still napping...

BASCOM: And the laundry?

SHAUN: The laundry is still being done... At this stage I'm still folding clothing — still feeding that ravenous washer... still getting the last weekend wash sorted out. (*Chuckles.*) This is going to take me into the afternoon.

By now it's 3:00 PM. I leave the laundry room and head up to the kitchen. There, I would take out whatever meat has to be thawed for dinner, and then head back down to the basement. Matt would be awake by now. I would make sure that he's not wet... make sure he's clean and take him to his high chair in the kitchen for a snack.

By now it's 3:15 and the kids would be home. When they come in they would grab snacks and head down to the basement. I would take Matt down to his playpen in the basement so that he can be with his brothers and sister. This would give me to break to finish off little things on the first floor like making sure that the living room is in order: that the cushions are in the right places, that there are no toys in the chairs; that the floor is clean... that nothing is obviously dusty... Then I would make sure that the sitting area with the fireplace is clean... that the grand stairway is clean. I would dry-wipe that.

By now it's going on to 4:00 PM., and Daisy is home from wherever she was —either playing tennis, or shopping. At this time the boys would most likely be playing outside while three-year-old Brittany and Matt are in the basement... Daisy would be in her private basement office... and the laundry is still going... Now it's going on to 5:00 PM. Dinnertime would be soon —6:00 —6: 30 P.M. I would head back to the kitchen and start preparing the evening meals...

BASCOM: And what might the evening meals be?

SHAUN: (*Shrugs.*) It could be oven-fried chicken, or breaded chicken breasts, or stake, or baked turkey breasts. With that, there might be mashed potatoes, pasta, rice and vegetables. While I'm cooking, I would take trips down to the laundry room... I would bring clothes into the kitchen so that I could continue to fold them while preparing dinner.

When dinner is ready, the boys would come up and help to set the table... making sure that the dishes and napkins... cutlery is laid out. They would help that way. Daisy would help me get the courses onto the table. Then I would sit with them and have dinner.

BASCOM: Where would the baby be at this time?

SHAUN: We'll bring his high chair close to the dining table and Daisy and I would take turns feeding him.

BASCOM: What about the husband? —Dr. D?

SHAUN: He'll be in some evenings for dinner —twice or three times a week. He was a surgeon and most days his job kept him at the hospital. If he would be coming home late, Daisy would leave his dinner in the oven... Anyway, by now dinner is over. The kids help to clear the table and scrape the leftovers into the garbage. Daisy would help to load the dishwasher.

Now it is about 7:15 P.M. or so and I'm still doing the laundry, but now it's also homework time. Even though I was not hired to be a governess or something like that, I would sometimes help the kids with their assignments...

Then I would tidy up Matt and prepare him for bed.

BASCOM: And what time is it now?

SHAUN: By now? By now it's about 8:30 PM or there about. I would bathe Brittany and the two younger boys— one seven, the other eight—and make sure they go to bed.

By now it's about 9:00 P.M. and I'm pooped. The laundry will continue tomorrow. I head up to my room on the third floor and collapse into the easy chair close to my bed. I would sit there a while and allow the tiredness to drain from my body. Then I would take a shower, change into my sleeping clothes, and hit my bed. There I would watch TV... think about my life, how good God was to me... and fall off to sleep...

CHAPTER II: 1994
The Summit Story Continues

SOLO TRIP BACK TO RAHWAY BY TRAIN

My first workweek ended on that Friday night. I looked forward to getting back to Rahway in order to rest a bit and see my cousins, Zan and Brandon. I lay in bed and thought of the journey back to Rahway. Dr. D would take me in his car to the Summit train station, where I would take the Gladstone line to Broad Street, Newark. From there I was going to catch a bus to Penn Station and a train to Rahway. In order to get to my uncle's home from there, I would have to walk—say a mile and a half; that's what they told me. I knew I would be okay; I had been always good at remembering directions.

Saturday morning came and I tried not to show the D's that I was eager to leave them. I was happy that I'd be free for a few days. The doctor's demeanor was bright as the sunshine gleaming on the icicles that hung from the bumper of the big Cadillac with four of the kids in the back seat.

"Are we ready, Shaun my dear?" he said cheerily.

"I am, Doctor D…"

"All aboard!" he said laughing, mimicking a train conductor.

On the way to the train station I was a little bit unsure I'd be able to find my way back to Rahway. I was a little apprehensive… fearful? I covertly sighed it away as the doctor chatted about how happy they all were to have me as nanny. In my head I heard my grandfather's voice: "Once you have an English tongue in your head —you can't get lost, Shawnee!" It consoled me —gave me a sudden boost of confidence. I thought, *I could also read signs! I'll be okay! I'll also make sure to use the information booths whenever I need to. I'll be okay.*

I said goodbye to Dr. D and the kids and boarded the train. It took a while to leave… seems I was very early. I thought of my mother. *What was she doing now? Boasting to a neighbor about her daughter being in the States and doing good?* I smiled to myself... shook my head slightly. That would not be like my mother. My dad! He would more be doing something like that amongst his friends and co-workers at the telecommunication corporation where he worked. I sat there and I thought of Carlton... *Is he thinking of me?*

A slight lurch —the train was pulling out. This was it. My chest tightened with apprehension. I watched the wintry landscape slip by, and settled into my seat hoping that the hypnotic sound of the train did not lull me to sleep.

The journey seemed longer than I had expected, but finally the intercom system announced, "Broad Street Station..."

The vast City of Newark was a great panorama of brownstones and factories and churches and office buildings below me. I took a great breath and prepared to get off.

I descended the platform and found myself on the busy streets, and in luck. There was a NJ Transit bus waiting and on its forehead were the words, *Penn Station*. I boarded it and paid seventy-five cents for a fifteen-minute ride to Penn Station. Once I got there, I headed for the information booth. ...

"Good morning... could you tell me what train do I take in order to get to Rahway, please?"

"A good morning to you, dear... You sound so mannerly you've made my day. Now... to get to Rahway you take those stairs there... —you see them?"

"Yes..."

"It will lead you to track four. That is where you're going to wait for the train for Rahway to pull in. Once it does and you board it, you'll be on your way..."

"Okay... —Thank you so very much..."

"Thank *you*..."

I headed off through throngs of people for the stair. The hustle and bustle that Saturday morning made me feel warm inside. Aside from the cold, I was somehow reminded of a Saturday morning in Georgetown back in my tropical Guyana. The anxiety about getting lost was rapidly fading.

Soon the train to Rahway arrived and I boarded it confidently. A young conductor smiled at me and I felt good inside. I was beginning to feel as though I were a regular on the Summit-to-Rahway commute. I settled into a comfortable window seat. I felt so more at ease. I was going home.

Less than three hours later, I arrived at the Rahway Train Station, and descended the stairs to the streets. I stood at an intersection and looked left and then right to get my bearings, so to speak, and in a rush it came to me. My lips were cold... my ears were beginning to ache. But what could I have done dressed the way I was dressed? Nothing else but will myself on.

After what seemed an eternity, I turned a corner and spotted my uncle's house. On entering the yard I prayed that someone would be up to let me in from the North Pole in my mind. I rang the bell with numbed fingers and waited.

Zanette, face flushed with excitement, greeted me. She let me in, shut the door on the chill, and I hugged her. She felt so warm.

"Cousin Shaun... you're so cold..."

"It's freezing out there." I said laughing —so glad to be finally back... so proud of myself for completing the journey all the way from the Summit Train Station, to Uncle David's home in Rahway.

· · ·

BASCOM: Bear with me Shaun... I need to go back to the day of the interview for the nanny job with the D's...

SHAUN: No problem.

BASCOM: You told me that the doctor and his wife were scheduled to go on a one-week vacation... they asked you if you think you'd be able to take charge of things in their absence... and you said 'yes'... but tell me honestly! What were you really saying inside of yourself?

SHAUN: (*Laughs lightly.*) The thought of being solely responsible for the security of the house and children was scary. To be honest I was filled with trepidation. I had *no* idea how I was going to take care of five kids and manage this humongous mansion. For that week the Doctor's mother was going to come over and help me with the kids, but when they told me she was 85 years old I wondered how much help would she be? To be honest I was caught off guard about the week thing, but I knew that if I had said that I wouldn't be able to accept that responsibility, I might not have gotten the job. Honestly? I was unsure, but showed no signs that I was.

BASCOM: So the doctor and his wife went off on their one-week vacation—

SHAUN: To Las Vegas...

BASCOM: And you took charge admirably until they returned...

SHAUN: (*Laughing lightly*.) Took charge admirably until they returned. I think that really endeared me to them.

. . .

I would always remember the D family with fondness. Daisy was a really fun person. She was actually born the same month as me —the same planet. So If I were to talk about what kind of person she was, I would say that she was a bit like me... but then she had all these kids. She loved them, but she was not really the mother type. I got the impression she didn't want to be around them much. So I became like their mom. Daisy was like this really free spirit. I remember that time when Matt started to speak. He began calling me Mom and I told him no —that I wasn't his mom. So I said to her, "Daisy, he's calling me Mom." But she didn't seem to mind. "So what, Shaun?" she said, shrugging it away. "He's got two moms... that's good!"

A few of times every week, Daisy worked on-call at the hospital. She also worked from her home office as a consultant and editor for an insurance company. Most of Daisy's time, however, was spent hanging out with other rich women —you know, doing whatever affluent people do... —play tennis... —go to beauty spas... decorate their homes... shop for themselves and kids... —plan vacations... —in short, Daisy had a ball spending her husband's money.

. . .

BASCOM: Spending the good doctor's money... Tell me a little about him.

SHAUN: Doctor D was a fun guy. He was a short, heavy-set man with a quick smile. He was actually half Puerto Rican and half Irish American. He was a people person. Even though he was a surgeon and worked a lot, he would still find time to cook his 'specials' for Daisy and the kids. He was light hearted —always joking... always laughing. One day he said to me... (*Smiles.*) He said, "Shaun com'on let's go to the park. I'll show you how to drive." And he'd take me to the park with all the kids in the backseat, and he would attempt to teach me top drive. They were going to give me a stick-shift car that Daisy drove —a Volvo. The very offer was such a thrill because I had never driven a car before. But how would I have been given the title and things like that? At that point in time I was beyond the extension of my visa and was undocumented. My papers were not legal anymore...

BASCOM: Speaking about paper work. You said they made you a sponsorship offer. How did it come up? What was the offer they made you exactly? —Who talked to you about it?

SHAUN: But before I get to that, I must tell you about how I got reconnected with my Aunt Desiree and met Nigel...

CHAPTER 12: 1994
The Summit Story Continues

RECONNECTING WITH MY AUNT DESIREE

A few months into working at the D's, the phone rings in Shaun's room after yet another seemingly endless day of what had become a recurring monotony of being a nanny and house-keeper. She reaches for it tiredly... wondering who it might be. It is well after nine...

"Hello?"

"Shaun?"

"Hi, Uncle David..."

"You sound tired..."

She chuckles. "That, I am..."

"Your aunt Desiree called me today..."

"Aunt Desiree? —I would love to see her!"

"That's why I'm calling you. She's working as a nanny too —and not very far from you. She over in Millburn... right here in New Jersey —I told her you have a job in Summit and she's really excited about meeting you..."

"I'm excited too..."

"You have pen and paper handy? I'll give you her phone number, okay?

. . .

Ten-year old Shaun sits with the other children under her grandparent's house in Phoenix Park: the new housing scheme built on land claimed from acres of mangroves in from the shores of the muddy-faced Demerara River over which the shoreline of shipping wharfs are seen. Her aunt Desiree stands serious-faced before the little class on wooden benches. "Look at me, Aunt Desiree! Look at me!" little Shaun chants within her mind. She knows the answer. Her aunt had asked what the golden color on the national flag represented. Shaun knows the answer...

. . .

Shaun chuckles to herself as she looks at the telephone number for her Aunt Desiree. "Shaun," she whispers. "You've come a long way..." She smiles as she reaches for the telephone, dials the number, and someone answers...

"Aunt Desiree?"

"Shaun?"

And they were laughing together.

"Oh my God I'm so happy my niece!"

"So how are you doing, Aunt Desiree?"

"I'm doing fine, girl —and I'm working not too far from where you are ..."

"Uncle David told me... —Millburn?"

"Yes —that's not far from where you are... —I'm doing this little nanny job —taking care of an old lady, you know... These are the kinds of jobs you have to do until..."

"I know, Aunt Desiree... I'm working as a nanny too..."

"Well you know we have to get together," her aunt was saying.

Shaun felt a tad uncomfortable. This was an aunt that she always had regarded with awe... Aunt Desiree the serious teacher who would have rebuked her for her childhood transgressions and made her nervous. Now here they were talking over the phone —talking the way Shaun might have spoken to one of her girlfriends back home.

"When will you be off, Shaun?"

"Incidentally, this coming weekend I'll be off..."

"Me too —and this weekend I'll be going over to New York..."

"New York! —Wow!"

"Want to come with me?"

"Why not, Aunt Desiree? —So how are we going to meet? —I'm still getting a grip of traveling around here..."

"Okay... this is how we'll do it. You know how to get to the Newark, Penn Station?"

"Yes..."

"Once I meet you there, we'll take the Path train and we'll go to New York..."

"Okay..."

It was about the middle of summer when she spoke with her aunt. Prior to the conversation, however, it had continued to be winter in Shaun's heart. The invitation for her to go to New York brought home the warmth and sunshine to her. It had been all so timely. The euphoria of working with the D family had worn off. Little Matt wasn't a baby anymore and Shaun's status as an illegal resident wore heavily on her. A couple of weeks back she had sat below grassy dunes in Cape Cod with the D kids arrayed close to her. Before her the vast ocean waited below the distant sound of the surf and sea birds.

She remembered Cape Cod...

Deep trepidation courted her as she sat below those grassy dunes doing what countless immigrant women do for countless rich American families. This was not her American dream. This was not what she envisioned as her lot. The children she looked at were destined to grow into yet another batch of privileged white men and women destined to hire the earth's insignificance and ply them with minor comforts and paltry gifts in exchange for their very substance —their lives!

The thought that she would be going to New York filled her with a smile. As listened to her Aunt Desiree on the phone, she lay back in the bed provided for the D's maids. In her heart there was a smile. Somewhere from the summer night someone laughed and she thought of Carlton and back to that time when they were teenagers, when she had to be cautious whenever he came over on his bicycle to see her and her parents were out. She chuckled silently to remember her brother Glenn who acted as the lookout. He would ride back quickly on Carlton's bicycle to alert them that either mommy—or worse—daddy was on the way home.

"So where would we be staying in New York, aunt Desiree?'

"You remember teacher Marva?"

"Her daughter Simone and I were good friends, remember? Wow! ... I'm looking forward to seeing Simone..."

"We'll be staying with them in Brooklyn..."

CHAPTER 13: 1994

The Summit Story Continues

MEETING NIGEL

The rules of Russian roulette are simple: place a bullet in one of the chambers of a pistol, spin the cylinder, point the gun at your own head, and pull the trigger. If the player is still alive afterward, he passes the gun to the next player who repeats the process. The game would continue until someone died, or the players either sobered up or got so drunk they passed out.

BASCOM: And you and your aunt began going to Brooklyn...

SHAUN: Often. It became our thing. We would meet up, at head over to New York on weekends —Friday afternoons or Saturday mornings... —Fast forward to the Christmas of that year of '94: Guyanese always have house parties —people getting together... I had never gone to a party since I had come over... Thus far there had been no one in my life to take me any place like a club or something like that, but that Christmas I went to this house party in Brooklyn. A relative of Teacher Marva hosted it, and at this party were Simone's brothers and cousins. Anyway, I'm at this Old Years night party, and in the process of meeting people, I met Nigel...

BASCOM: Guyanese?

SHAUN: Yes, he was born back in Guyana but I didn't know him. He was Simone's cousin, and about my age range... *He* knew all my family but *I* did not know him. He had been here since whatever age he was... (*Shrugs.*) So we started to chitchat and it was kinda nice to have somebody kinda close to your age —he was older than me... but we started to talk... and his cousin later told me that he had just broken up with a girlfriend and that it would be nice for me to hang out with him... (*Shrugs.*) In a way, people started putting us together...

BASCOM: (*Chuckling.*) Matchmakers of the world unite!

SHAUN: (*Chuckles, then...*) So we began talking from then... It so happened that things quickly escalated into where we were dating... By now I learned the trains and could have gotten from Summit to New York on my own. I didn't have to wait on my aunt. She normally came off her job on Saturday, and I would already be in New York the day before. Then Nigel began driving from New York to get me...

BASCOM: He would come and pick you up from the D's and take you over to New York...

SHAUN: Yes...

BASCOM: Now! —Now! —At this point, I'm sure that Daisy or Doctor D is aware that there's a guy who's coming to pick up the nanny...

SHAUN: Well I introduced them both to Nigel because I became like family —like part of their home and it was only respectful to let them know who Nigel was... and they showed him a nice face —seemed they liked him. He would come by sometimes early and hang out and play with the kids and wait on me, you know, to get done on Friday afternoon... and then we'd head over back to New York. And spend the weekend...

But it so happened that the weekends ran into each other... and then one night after Nigel dropped me back to Summit... he began to talk... by now we were seeing each other for a while... and he said, "You know what, Shaun... why don't we get married? Don't you think that would make sense? —For both of us?" ...(*Sighs.*) I remember I said to him, "Nigel... I must be open and honest with you... I have a boyfriend back home and I promised him I'd return to him... for him.

BASCOM: That you already had a commitment... —And what Nigel said?

SHAUN: It didn't seem to put off him off... He reminded me that he was a citizen... "I could help you..." he said to me, "You know what? —You'll learn to love me —I don't care who you have back home..." He told me that all he knows was that he loves me and he would do anything to help me... And I said to him, "But how would it look to your family? —I don't want your family thinking I'm using you or anything like that..." But he was adamant that he was his own man and that he loved me and that they were going to have to live with whatever choices he made as a man. (*She sighs.*) The next day Daisy and I were in the basement... the kids had gone to school... and she said to me, "Well, how is Nigel —How are things going? —How was the weekend?" ...Asked me if I had a good time... (*Chuckles in reminiscence.*) It was always a bit awkward whenever Daisy questioned me about Nigel because she and her husband knew that I had a boyfriend back home —a relationship to which I had told them I was committed... plus Carlton continued to call me at the D's house. So, that morning in the basement Daisy and I had a kind of heart-to-heart talk.

· · ·

"Shaun..." Daisy D said. "You look a bit... —how must I put it? Preoccupied? ... Want to talk about it?"

Shaun sighed as she folded one of the doctor's shirts. "Nigel is proposing... for us to get married..."

Daisy said nothing for a thoughtful while, then, "Shaun... are you sure you want to do something like that?"

She shrugged. "I really don't know, Daisy..."

"You really shouldn't rush into something like this —even though I do understand your circumstances..."

"It's not a matter of *rushing* into anything!" She took a covert intake of breath to calm herself and then continued: "If I don't do it... I won't be able to stay here... legally..."

"Shaun..." Daisy said gently.

She felt Daisy's hand on hers.

"We can sponsor you, Shaun... —think about it! Other people have done it for their nannies... The doctor and I were speaking about it... we *can* sponsor you... Doctor D and I spoke about sponsoring you..."

Shaun said nothing.

Music filtered from Daisy's basement office Where Shaun had helped her quite recently with her month's accounts and discovered that a pair of Daisy's shoes was more twice what Daisy paid her per week... that Daisy's monthly bills was way more than she would make in two years working for the D's.

"Once you agree, we can file for you," Daisy was saying, "and you're going to be here with the kids —and the kids will grow up... and you'll always be with us..."

Bitterness filled Shaun's heart.

"Just think about it, Shaun."

"I'm going to think about it, Daisy... —thanks."

. . .

The entire Summit area was an affluent suburban, Caucasian enclave, and I guess most of the nannies were undocumented women from other countries —and a sure way for those rich families to ensure that nannies stayed with them for a very long, was to offer them sponsorship... and it would have taken them ten years to do that for me...

Ten years...

I looked at ten years... (*Shakes her head.*) Unacceptable. I had spoken to other nannies and had picked up a few things through the grape vine, you know —also from listening to WLIB radio where I picked news and issues as it affected Caribbean immigrants. I learned that sponsorship took time. At that time, it would have taken the D's some ten years to make me legal —and not from the time I would have been here, but from the time *they* chose to file whatever papers that were required to begin the process. I looked at ten years of my life doing what I do in Daisy's house ... —I couldn't do it! I was almost into a year of working with them and a deep disappointment in self had set in. By that time Nigel was sort of proposing to me and Daisy was hinting that they would sponsor me, but there was one thing I was sure of: that I was *not* going to commit my fertile life as a twenty-four year old young woman to a ten-year indentureship of domesticated drudgery for a Green Card... —no way on God's green earth!

The struggle for me was, that I had come from a background where I was independent. I worked for a national financial institution back in my county. So working as a nanny in Summit, New Jersey was very difficult to resolve even though I understood my immigration status and is limitations. A lot of things were going through my mind. There were two clear-cut choices: ten years doing something that I knew was eating me from the inside out, or getting married to Nigel even though I had made a commitment to this man back home: that I was going to return and take up where I had left off with him.

At that point in time, I continued getting letters and phone calls from him, and he would tell me how much he loved and missed me. He was asking how he could have visited —pressing me to receive him as a holiday guest, and all this was happening as the situation between Nigel and myself became more serious. And then Nigel decided to move out of his parents' home in order to be closer to me.

· · ·

BASCOM: He was serious about having a real relationship with you...

SHAUN: He was sincere about it, yes... So, in '95 Nigel moved to Summit where I was and we got a little space in a communal house where people rented rooms. We rented a small attic room where he would come and take me on a weekend...

BASCOM: How small was this room?

SHAUN: It was so small we couldn't get a bed in there. All we had was a mattress... —so that's where we lived...

At this time he would be driving from Summit to go to his job in New York. Meantime he had completed a course in being a Licensed Practical Nurse and had acquired enough certificates to work in a Nursing Home as a Nursing Assistant. But he wasn't doing that. So I said to him, "What about if you get a little side job or move over here to New Jersey and go into being a Nursing Assistant fully? —And from that you can move up to studying to be a Registered Nurse —"

BASCOM: And he took your advice...

SHAUN: He did. He left the mailroom job he had been doing at a bank in New York and found a job over in New Jersey...

BASCOM: I guess that at this point there must have been some family friction.

SHAUN: Not much, you know... Nigel was his own man. There might have been some sort of feeling due to the fact that he moved from his mother's house... I can't recall any drama to speak about. His family was nice people... his mother and I had a very good relationship —his mom liked me... his dad liked me too... (*Shrugs.*) I'm sure there were people who were concerned —or I should say 'afraid' that I might have been 'using' Nigel for a Green Card...

BASCOM: So it *was* a good thing you told Nigel everything about Carlton...

SHAUN: Told him the entire history of Carlton and myself...

BASCOM: And the fact that you told him everything is an indication that you had actually fallen in love with him...

SHAUN: (*Shrugs.*) I guess...

BASCOM: Anyway, let's continue with him and you living together...

SHAUN: He found a job in a nursing home in West Caldwell... It was around that time that my Aunt Desiree, Nigel and myself, decided to come together and rent a proper apartment in New Jersey... So I began talking to Daisy about an apartment, and one of her girlfriend told me about Montclair, New jersey —about it being a good place for me to have an apartment, you know, that it was a good place for immigrants —a culturally mixed community where everybody got along... (*Chuckles.*) 'A kind of Sesame-Street kind of place.' Her actual words... Daisy's girlfriend told me it would have been a very good place for me to rent an apartment...

So having told Nigel, I told my aunt Desiree. They all felt it was a good idea, so I got into the papers, looked up a realtor, and they helped us find an apartment.

CHAPTER 14: 1995

The Montclair, New Jersey, Story

If you find yourself craving quiet suburban life with sprawling lawns and leisurely shopping on a quaint Main Street, Montclair is a utopia awaiting mere miles from New York City. Aptly nicknamed "New Jersey's Florence," this town has everything from minor league baseball to art museums without losing its small-town suburban feel.

It was a huge second floor with two bedrooms... bathroom... big dining room... big kitchen —to me it was perfect! The guy who owned it was a Haitian name was Danny. He understood the difficulties new immigrants experience in finding their footing in America, and we were lucky to see him that very day. He agreed to let us have the apartment. Even though it was five of us—Nigel and me, my aunt, her daughter LaToya and her husband Joe—Danny adjusted the rent to help us out.

Later I went back let Daisy know that everything was going well and that we found an apartment. She and Dr. D were happy for me.

Nigel rented a U-haul and brought over much of his stuff from his room in New York —stuff that couldn't fit into the little attic in Summit, and we began moving into the apartment in Montclair.

. . .

BASCOM: What year are we now in?

SHAUN: Oh —this is still ninety-five...(*Sighs.*) a very difficult year for me. I had to make decisions... whether I should accept sponsorship from the D's and preserve my relationship with Carlton... or continue with Nigel and marry him for a Green Card... but deep inside of me it was more than that. I guess I realized what Nigel was feeling for me was real and...

I was seeing him as someone I truly wanted to take care of... (*Shakes her head.*) Ninety-five was one very trying year for me...

BASCOM: Let's jump ahead a bit. When exactly did you marry Nigel?

SHAUN: I married Nigel in January '96. After I had a talk with Daisy and told her that I was forego them sponsoring me, Nigel and I got married.

BASCOM: Tell me about the ceremony...

SHAUN: We went to New York one morning and did one of those Justice of the peace things, you know... Back in Guyana we call them 'Registrar marriages.' Go to the place; go through the signings —(*Shrugs.*) — that's it. My girlfriend Lynn was a witness... It went well... Afterwards we went to I-hop for breakfast. ... People didn't know Nigel and I got married —we didn't tell anybody anything. They found out later on... and then something happened that tested my faith...

BASCOM: What happened?

SHAUN: My grandma died a few months later... What hurt me was that I could not go to her funeral. It tore me up. I loved my grandma so much. She was my heart and soul. When I was leaving Guyana she had said to me: "I'm so happy you're going to America, my grand-child... but when you're coming back I want you to bring a watch for me —that is all your grandmother want: a wrist watch..." (*Sighs.*) That winter was the biggest snowfall I would have seen for a long time to come...(*Shakes her head.*) After I heard that she died, I went out in the snow and bought that watch. I took whatever I had and I bought my grandma a little watch with tiny diamonds around the face... and told my aunt who was going home, to put it in Grandma's coffin for me...

BASCOM: I know I'm guilty of making you jump back and forth, but right now I think you, Nigel, your aunt Desiree and her family are living in the Haitian guy's apartment, and that is nineteen ninety-five...

SHAUN: Correct. We lived together at that apartment in ninety-five, but after Nigel and I got married, we eventually moved and rented our own little place in Chestnut Street, not too far away...

CHAPTER 15: 2007
Oklahoma

THE MORNING AFTER THE CONVENTION'S LAST DAY

Her cell phone's alarm was going off. Shaun groped for it and thumbed it off. She looked over to the other bed. Good. Her mom and aunt slept on. Identity Theft Risk Management specialist Shaun Stephenson sat up yawning from her Best Western hotel bed. She twisted her body towards the window that faced the verandah overlooking the swimming pool. Carefully she got up and parted the curtains. Gorgeous Oklahoma morning. She thought it was a great looking day to fly out for New Jersey. The wind blew gently through the trees glimpsed beyond the hotel. Birds chirped. Peaceful... She yawned again... stretched.

The Convention ended the night before and what an ending it had been. The informal coming together of Executive Director Russell Peden along with other Legal Eagle Team leaders to celebrate the end of three very fruitful days of learning and sharing was also a lot of fun.

Shaun smiled to herself to remember... She and Maryetta were there together amidst the sipping and chatting and dancing.

She remembered...

They bumped into Millionaire Club Member, Carmilo Flores wearing his special ring, encrusted with diamonds. "Hello, Mr. Flores," Shaun said. "It is an honor meeting you. I must congratulate you on your commendable achievement."

"Thank you, my dear... —and I'm having the pleasure to be speaking to...?"

"My name is Shaun Stephenson... —from New Jersey..."

"How are you, my friend?" he said.

"Extraordinary!" she answered.

She remembered how floored he seemed by her response, and how he was further surprised when she said, "Mr. Flores, I'd like to take a picture wearing your ring. I know I'll soon be joining you at the top. I just want to know how the ring on my finger will feel."

Without hesitation he took it off and slipped it on her finger.

"Look at me, Maryetta! —Wow! ...This will soon be me..."

"It's just a matter of time, my dear," Carmilo Flores said. "It's just a matter of time..."

At that little event she literally rubbed shoulders with Pre-paid Legal's best-of-the best; even 'Mama Fran' whose full name was Fran Alexander was there. She was with Pre-Paid Legal Incorporated from its early years and was considered a legend. This was a woman who had been able build a great team through hard work and determination. Her rags-to-riches story is legend. It was great to talk with her —to feel and share her passion, sincerity, and vision for her PPLSI and the Legal Eagles team.

"I'm so glad I came," Shaun Stephenson yawned and whispered. In her heart she was ecstatic —ready to get back and expand on her business. Shaun's flight out of Will Rogers World Airport for the trip back to New Jersey was scheduled to leave at twelve-noon.

She yawned again... turned, and got herself a bathrobe from the room's little closet. Her Aunt Bridgett stirred.

"Shaun?" Alarm flared briefly in her aunt's eyes.

"It's alright, Aunt Bridgett...go back to sleep..."

"What time is it?" her mom mumbled.

"It's only about five forty-five, Mom. ... Go back to sleep both of you... I'm going to wake you when it's time for breakfast, okay?"

She stepped out onto the veranda that overlooked the pool and felt the Oklahoma breeze on her face. She inhaled deeply. The two-day, Pre-Paid Legal Convention was over. Shaun was experiencing rejuvenation. It had been an event she would always remember.

She looked down at the rectangular patch of slightly undulating, aquamarine water beginning to reflect the morning sun. As yet there were no takers for the poolside tables and chairs. No swimmers, only the man with the reddish brown hair as he floated on a yellow-green inflated raft. In his floating with his eyes closed, he seemed as tranquil as Shaun's mind. She breathed easily. The color of the man's inflatable reminded her of the one her dad floated on, aback her Mantua, New Jersey home where he had stayed a while before returning to Guyana to die.

Just like that she found herself remembering the very first

time her dad came to America. He had been so ill, it could have been said that he was at death's door.

She closed her eyes.

. . .

On his very first trip to the U.S. her dad was picked up from the John F. Kennedy airport and brought to the home of a close Trinidadian friend of hers. After work Shaun picked her dad up. It was the first time she was seeing him after he had given her away to Carlton at her wedding back in Guyana.

Despite the veiled animosity between them, she felt very sad when she looked at her dad. He had had lost so much weight, it was hard matching him to the man she always knew. The elegant, charismatic, playboy of a man her father had always been was now a tall, skinny man with darkened skin and jaundiced eyes. She trembled inside; she saw a dying man.

She gazed down at the swimming pool and remembered...

As she made the two-hour drive to her Maple Shade apartment with him by her side, he said little, but slept most of the time. And most of the time he seemed as though trying to hide his pain.

"You okay, Dad?"

"Yes... I'm okay..."

She sighed covertly. *His pride will be the death of him!*

When they finally arrived at her town house apartment, her mom came out to help. Her dad seemed too weak to walk on his own, and she saw the panic in her mom's eyes. They managed to get him to the door and then discovered that he could not climb the stair to the second floor of her apartment.

She looked at her mom who seemed close to tears.

"Mom... What are we going to do? How are we going to get Dad upstairs?"

"We can call a neighbor," she said.

"Mommy, this is not Guyana, people here don't get involved like that..."

"Don't fight," her father said, settling himself slowly to sit at the bottom of the stair. Then he began to pull himself up to sit on the next tread above; and bit by bit he worked himself backwards until he was sitting at the top of the stair...

Shaun remembered that was when she burst into tears.

They helped him to his feet and Shaun led them to her room.

"Mom... you and Dad could use my bedroom. It's larger and you'll be more comfortable... —I'll use your bedroom..."

The very next day she took him to a doctor in Pennsauken, New Jersey, who she felt sure, misdiagnosed her father. She requested a copy of the blood work, saw that his white count was way up, and saw too that the doctor had given him an anti-biotic for bronchitis. From all appearances she was sure that her father wasn't suffering from anything like that.

They took him home, things only got worse for him, and Shaun rushed him to the Emergency room At Kennedy Health Systems in Cherry Hill, New Jersey. They admitted him immediately and hooked him up to several IVs.

It took the doctor over eight days to figure our what was wrong with her dad; and while they were in that process of diagnosis, Shaun was doing her own on-line research on her father's symptoms, and had come up with Primary Sclerosis Cholangitis —a diagnosis that was eventually confirmed as correct by the hospital's gastroenterologist.

"Mrs. Stephenson..." he said. "There is nothing more we, at the Kennedy Health Systems, can do for your dad. He needs to get on a liver transplant list. I would recommend that you have him admitted to the Lady of Lords Hospital where you have Dr. B —the best there is in this field..."

Shaun remembered...

That was after her dad had been at The Kennedy Health Center for ten days where they had been continually feeding antibiotics through the IV system to flush his system. They said that his bile ducts were severely blocked.

Shaun remembered the day she arrived at The Kennedy and a nurse told her that her dad was going to be discharged that very day. "I'm going to give you a Prescription that the doctor has left... and a copy of the diet he needs to be on..."

She saw her that her dad was happy to leave; he never liked being sick, and he never cared for hospitals.

"Man, I'm glad they're discharging me," he said weakly.

"Okay, Dad," she said as she packed his clothes. "We're leaving now, but..." She shook her head. "I have to get you in another hospital!"

"But I alright..."

"Dad!" she snapped. "You're *not* all right! —You're a *very* ill man!"

Shaun remembered...

That very day she began to think of what she had to do in order to save her father's life. She was determined to get him the medical help he needed. She knew that the medication he was on would help him for only so long.

Back at her apartment he continued to suffer. He would have itchy breakouts on his back, belly and eventually over his entire body. She remembered that very early morning when he awoke scratching himself. Her mom was home from her live-in job and filled the bathtub with cool water, added *Aveeno bath*, and had him sit in the tub...

Shaun remembered...

She soaked and rubbed her dad's back to help cool him down; after a while he said that he felt better and was able to go back to sleep.

Soon after that episode Shaun refused to linger and contacted the Lady of Lords Hospital, and got a hold of Dr. B. She spoke to him and he agreed to see her dad. She made sure that she had all medical records and was fully prepared for this visit. Her mom accompanied them. The kind doctor welcomed them; Shaun introduced her dad, and began telling the doctor everything she knew about her father's illness.

"Well, well, young women..." Dr. B said as he read the medical material she had brought, "I must say that I am quite impressed." He looked at my dad. "Mr. Harry," he said. "You're blessed to have a daughter such as this..." He continued poring over the documents and then he cleared his throat lightly.

"Okay, Mrs. Stephenson..." he said.

"You can call me, Shaun, doctor..."

"Okay... Shaun, we need to have some X-rays taken of your dad... but from what I'm reading here... surgery is recommended for your dad's condition..." He turned to my dad. "Mr. Harry..." He nodded. "You'll soon be right as rain."

"There are X-rays for him at the Kennedy Health Center, doctor... —I will request them."

"That will be perfect, Shaun…"

She remembered her father was smiling and her mom was holding his hand.

"This operation will have to be done at the Temple University Hospital in Pennsylvania…"

Shaun remembered wondering about how they'd be able to afford the procedure. She thought of the Company her father worked for back in Guyana. She thought, *He has worked for years with T.C. he therefore has money owed him for medical emergencies under Guyana's National Insurance Program.*

She made contacted with the T.C. Company back in Guyana, and told them of her father's condition. To her dismay, none of the Company's executives were prepared to make any fund available to help with her dad's medical expenses.

In the meantime she secured the X-Rays but had to get them to Dr. B and he was then at the hospital in Pennsylvania where she had never driven to before. She went to Map Quest, input the hospital's address and started out for the Temple University Hospital. With directions in hand she found it easily. Dr. B went over the X-rays and told her that he would be able to proceed with the operation on her father once funding for the procedure was found.

"You know I would love to help your dad, Shaun…" He shrugged. "If it were up to me I would help your dad out…"

"I understand…"

In the end she could not assure payment for the procedure and had to look elsewhere. In the meantime her dad was barely hanging on with the help of the medication prescribed by the doctor from the Kennedy Health Systems Center.

"What are we going to do, Mom?"

"Why not call your aunt?"

She remembered.

She called her dad's sister and told her what was happening. "Aunt… I need help taking care of Dad since I have to be flying home to bring my husband back to America."

"Okay, Shaun; but where do we stand with Patrick?"

She told her aunt, and they spoke at length about what they might do. In the end it was decided that they took her dad to the UMDNJ —the University of Medicine and Dentistry of New Jersey.

She remembered praying like she never prayed before that they admitted him. Before she, her mom, her dad, and her aunt Desiree left for the hospital, they told him not to say anything on his own behalf. He agreed, and they began the drive to the UMDNJ emergency room. It was a Saturday evening.

They pulled up to the emergency block and Shaun was once again silently praying fore her dad's admittance. He went through Triage and got a bed. The emergency room was packed that night so they had to wait several hours before anyone came to look at him. Finally a doctor came...

"Hi... My name is Dr. J." She sounded genuinely pleasant. "Who do we have here?"

"This is my father," Shaun said.

"You have an accent," the doctor said.

"You too," her Aunt Desiree said. "You're Jamaican..."

Dr. J smiled. "I am —and you are Guyanese?"

"Yes," her Aunt Desiree said, and indicated Shaun and her mom. "This is my niece and her mom, and this is my brother..."

"So what your problem, sir?" Dr. J said to my dad.

He looked at Shaun and she looked at him. She hoped he did not speak. She knew how very rapidly he spoke —especially when he was uncomfortable.

"Dr. J," Shaun said in earnest. "I will be honest with you. My dad here is very ill. He has Primary Sclerosis Cholangitis; we found out that he may need an operation, but we can't afford it..."

"We don't have that kind of money," added her Aunt Desiree, "so we came here to get some help..."

"I understand..." Dr. Jessica said, nodding. "You know what? I will see if I can help you out —I will speak to the doctor in charge..."

"Thank you, Dr. J," her aunt said.

Dr. J squeezed her wrist gently, and slipped away.

Her mom whispered, "We all got to pray..."

Shaun remembered...

They waited a while longer and then Dr. J returned smiling.

Shaun remembered how happy she felt.

"We're going to admit him," Dr. J said, "but he won't have a bed on the floor until later..."

Shaun remembered her tears of gratitude...

"Thank you... thank you so very, very much," her mom said to Dr. J.

"Our people have to help each other," Dr. J said. "Your dad will be okay. It was nice meeting you," she said and was gone.

Shaun kissed her dad. "We'll be back tomorrow to see you, okay?"

"Thank you my daughter," he said, and then turned to his sister with tears in his eyes. "Thank you, my sister..."

There were tears in her aunt's eyes also.

Shaun remembered... Her mom hugged her dad, and she seemed reluctant to let him go...

· · ·

The next day, medical staff at UMDNJ, armed with all the records from the previous hospital, ran a battery of tests on her dad. They did a liver biopsy among other things, quickly diagnosed his illness, and began treating him. Within a few days he began to look better. They cleared his bile docks and the functioning of his system improved remarkably. No surgery was required, but the doctor advised a radical change of her dad's life style —especially as it related to what he ate and drank.

"Understand! Your dad's condition has no known cure, but if he takes care of himself he can live a long time."

Eight days later her dad—back to eighty percent of himself—was discharged with strict instructions about his diet and a regimen of medication prescribed.

Shaun remembered how much the medical bill was, and thought of her mom in the hotel room behind her. She mom took care of the expensive prescriptions. It was for the man she loved.

Her dad stayed the remainder of time with his sister and flew back to Guyana a new and healthy man —vowing to turn away from his previous life of debauchery and to do right by his family in the aftermath of having faced death.

Shaun sighed as she remembered her dad's last years...

He reneged on all his promises, returned to his former way of living, had a reversion of his sickness back in Guyana, and died in fall of 2006.

She looked at her watch; it was time for breakfast.

CHAPTER 16: 1996

The Montclair Story Continues

CHESTNUT STREET

---

76 Chestnut was the second house on the street from the corner of Fullerton. It was a four-family duplex painted cream with brown shutters. It stood out because of the large bougainvillea in the yard.

Shaun, back from doing a bit of light shopping, pushed open the little gate with a free hand and started up the short concrete path, bordered with immaculate flower beds. It led to a six-tread stair that would usher her to a porch divided by a wooden grill. The door on the left would usher her up to the apartment she and Nigel had recently rented from an elderly Jamaican woman whom had started calling her 'honey,' and treating her like a long lost granddaughter. Shaun didn't mind. She liked Mrs. Hughes too.

Shaun turned to the sound of a ball thumping along the sidewalk she had just left. A group of young men were coming by, no doubt heading over to the Montclair High School basketball court. One of the boys nodded a good morning to her. Another sniggered. Shaun smiled, opened the front door and entered the duplex. The low thumping of jazz rhythms and the sound of a jazz trumpet came softly through the door of the apartment below. She started up the stair that led to a door that would usher her into her apartment.

She unlocked the door and was immediately into the kitchen of her apartment. Its cream walls reminded her of home. She headed to the four-person dining table with the very tropical tablecloth Nigel had chosen at the discount store in Watchung Avenue and rested the ten-pound bag of rice and the four cans of evaporated milk onto it. The dining set was arrayed not far from the stove, the refrigerator, and the microwave. She opened the freezer and deposited the whole chicken she had bought and then headed off to the bedroom. She was tired from the week at Daisy's and would have settled for a sofa or a love seat before any silly show on TV but the living room was bare. In time she would be able to acquire some furniture.

Shaun lay back in bed and closed her eyes. Carlton shimmered and materialized. He would call to speak to her —to tell her how much he loved her and missed her... how much he wished she were back in Guyana with him... how confused he was that she seemed so preoccupied... how difficult he was finding it just to talk to her on the phone... how much he was hurting.

But how could he have known how much she too was hurting deep inside because of the truth? —That she had begun dating, living with, and had just recently married another man.

But Carlton sensed that something was amiss with their relationship. He wrote and told her as much. He said he couldn't help but believe she was jerking him around, and that if she was, she should be honest about it, and call their relationship quits.

. . .

She sighed, got up, and walked over to the sole bedroom window that faced the front gate and Chestnut Street. For a wistful moment she contemplated the brilliant-red hibiscus flowers that stood out from the crotons, the roses and the marigolds. Mrs. Hughes her landlady had planted the flaming flowers because it reminded her of Jamaica.

Shaun looked beyond the front yard. As she gazed out—seemingly oblivious of the trees-lined street... the tennis court and Montclair high school parking lot—she thought of home.

The sound of a door closing below brought her back to Montclair. The small, gray-haired gentleman who lived alone in the apartment below emerged in a beige-colored sweater and a little black case in one hand. A trumpet? He walked down the short pathway, opened the gate gently, closed it back, turned left on the sidewalk, and soon disappeared towards Fullerton Street.

"Shaun!" she said to herself. "You did what you had to do! Okay? Someday you will make it up to Doods!" She sighed and whispered, "There's no turning back!"

She turned and retraced her steps to the bed where he sat and looked around. She was making progress. *Soon I'll be able to leave Daisy's and work legally... soon I'll be able to study —to take a course in business in order to stand at the base of the corporate ladder with my face upwards.* And then she was whispering to herself, "I'm going to make it here in America. I have a way of getting things done... I *have* a way of getting things done... and things, good things, have a way of coming to me, and I *know* good things will continue to come my way. ...Look how easy I got this apartment. ...It was as if God wanted me to get it..."

She had taken a day off from Daisy for a realtor to show her and Nigel a few places available for renting. The first place they were taken to is a duplex in Chestnut Street where there was an apartment for rent. An elderly Black woman let them in. Her name was Mrs. Hughes, and she was Jamaican. When she heard Shaun's accent she surmised Shaun too was from the Caribbean. "Where you from" she asked.

Shaun told her. Mrs. Hughes squeezed Shaun's hand warmly but surreptitiously as she led the group to see the vacant apartment in the duplex she owned.

The moment Shaun saw the space she liked it: the kitchen... the bedroom... the neat little living room... She *liked* it. She was wondering if she and Nigel would be able to afford it, however.

The realtor guy entered the bathroom to look it over and the landlady pinched her covertly, drew close and whispered in her ear, 'If you like the apartment, don't tell them. Just call me back and me and you going to talk, okay?"

· · ·

BASCOM: What was *that* all about?

SHAUN: The woman didn't put her apartment through any realtor agency for rent! She didn't know how *they* knew she had a vacant apartment. And there this man was —walking into the old lady's house with prospective tenants as though the woman's house was listed his agency. So she gave me the wink for me to deal directly with her.

So, just for the sake of appearances Nigel and I went with the realtor guy and looked at a few other places before telling him that we were going to get back to him.

BASCOM: And then you called Mrs. Hughes...

SHAUN: Yes, and she told me to come over when I had the time.

BASCOM: When did you go over?

SHAUN: I went over right away —walked over there by my-self. It wasn't very far from the old apartment where I was with my aunt and her family. Nigel wasn't with me because he was at work. When I got there Mrs. Hughes invited me in, showed me the apart-ment again, and said, "I like you and your husband, so I'm going to rent you'all the place." I asked her how much rental was going to be. She told me sev-en-twenty a month. I told her that I couldn't afford seven-twenty. She asked me what we could afford and I told her six hundred. And she said, "Okay, be-cause of you I will take the six..."

BASCOM: And thus began the Chestnut Street, chapter... So how did things go from then?

SHAUN: Being in our own apartment was okay...but then there were so many other issues that I had to con-front daily, and most of it was due to me growing very disillusioned with the nanny job.

BASCOM: Disillusionment from being a nanny and maid.

SHAUN: You know... merely reflecting on that time challenges me not to be bitter about the Daisy D's of this world. (*Shakes her head.*) A breed of rich women who re-fuse to find the time clean their own homes and take care of their children... a breed of rich women who somehow believe that the only reason people like myself —Third World women—come to America is in order to be nannies and maids, and that we should not try to hurt ourselves aspiring to be anything else. (*Chuckles.*) Why would a 'nanny' want to leave and follow a dream?

BASCOM: And that was your problem with Daisy.

SHAUN: (*Nods.*) That was my problem with Daisy. Being there was becoming unbearable, Mr. Bascom. It was just too much work! I was really tired of it —and it wasn't as if I had gotten a raise since I started with these people. (*Sighs.*) Around April of that year—and that is after Nigel and I started living in Chestnut Street—I looked in the papers and there was another opening for a nanny in Summit. This woman was expecting and she knew that she would need someone to look after the baby, and she was going to pay me four hundred and fifty dollars a week and she lived not too far from where Daisy was. I went on the interview. When I came back and told Daisy—you know—that I was going to move on...

BASCOM: She didn't take it well...

SHAUN: That was like a no-no for her. It was like, "What are you thinking Shaun? —You're just going to leave us like this to go and work right across from where we live? —Do you know how this would affect the children? —How it would affect Matt?" She thought she was pulling the right strings because Matt said his first words with me... Matt walked with me... And that night the kids came to my room and they were crying and begging me not to leave...

SHAUN: And you stayed on.

SHAUN: I stayed on, but things got much more difficult, since they were expecting me to do more work because they had given me a raise.

CHAPTER 17: 1996

The Montclair Story Continues

THE TEMPORARY RESIDENT CARD

One Saturday morning she came home from the D's and discovered that her temporary resident card had arrived in the mail. She was upset that Nigel did not tell her about it. "Nigel! —How could you do this? Jeeze! —Yesterday I called and asked you if anything came in the mail for me and you said no!"

"I just wanted to surprise you, Shaun... I didn't know you would have taken it like this..."

"It's like you cheated me!"

"Shaun... I really don't see how. If I had told you it came, you would have been coming home filled with..." His voice trailed off.

"Excitement! Exactly."

"Hey, man I'm sorry..."

"Don't worry about it, Nigh... I understand..."

She carefully opened the very official envelope and her card was there.

"There you go... your Temporary Resident Card..." He put an arm around her shoulders gently. "You're halfway there..."

She sat in a dining chair and suddenly felt wretched. Why wasn't she as happy as she had thought she would have been? This was significant! After all those weeks of anxiety —of joyful anticipation —of calling home to Nigel almost daily to find out if anything had come in the mail for her. After all those thoughts of the many places she would go in search of the kind of work she knew was capable of doing... After all that, the Temporary Resident Card was finally in her hand... and here she sat —filled with a strange solemnity she could not understand. A lump came to her throat.

"What is it, baby?"

"Maybe... maybe it's just sad to see what people have to go through to be here..."

"You mean what you had to give up to stay in America..." He nodded. "I know."

She got up and hugged him tightly. "Thanks, Nigh..."

"You don't have to thank me, Shaun..." He caressed her back. "If it comes to that, I can thank you too..."

"I feel so grateful to you... for what you did for me..."

And in her heart of hearts she wanted to apologize for not loving him.

CHAPTER 18: 1996
The Montclair Story Continues

THE NIGHT OF THE SKUNK

Nigel turned in bed saw that she was awake. "You okay, Shaun?"

"Yeah," she said in a small voice.

He sat up and hugged her. "What's bothering you?"

"I'm thinking about Daisy..." She shook her head. "I don't want to be there any longer. I'm tired of doing that kind of work; I'm beginning to hate myself for allowing them to use me like this!"

"You have your Temporary Card, now..." he said. "Soon you'll find a real job. Don't stress about the D's..."

She allowed him to cuddle her back to bed. Soon he was snoring.

She gazed at the ceiling as a car rushed by in the fore dawn stillness. The smell of a skunk seeped in lightly. Maybe it was in Mrs. Hughes summer garden aback the duplex where tomatoes, eggplants, and herbs grew in the shade of an apple tree.

. . .

By the summer of '96 she had had it up to her neck with being Daisy's nanny. The Cape Cod vacation was the tipping point. Daisy, her sisters and their kids were vacationing together —and it wasn't as if they had each walked with their respective nannies. Shaun was also saddled with the care of Daisy's sister's kids. It was hard work while their moms, White and privileged, basked in luxurious self-indulgence.

It wasn't right.

It wasn't right, even though months before the vacation, it was Daisy and her husband whom had arranged that she got first choice of quality used furniture from a house sale of one of their suburban friends who moving Florida. It was not right even though they had given her an extra two hundred dollars to afford the few bits of living room furniture and a floor TV. And even though Dr. D loaded the things she bought into his oversized Lincoln Navigator and brought it all the way to Chestnut Street, her continuing life as a nanny and maid in the D's house was not right! After all the D's probably thought they had done for her, Shaun just wanted them to become a fond memory, for she had grown attached to the kids, and the kids to her. It wasn't going to be easy to say goodbye. This was part of what was troubling her.

A month ago she would have left, but thought to do it after four of the kids would have gone off on vacations: Brittany with her Granny in Greece, and three of the boys with their father in Puerto Rico. She calculated that it would have been easy on the kids to return and not find her. She reasoned that it would hurt them a bit... —that they may cry a bit, but find themselves once again after the new nanny walks into the kitchen. There would always be nannies for rich American families.

Then the day of the children's departure came. Brittany hugged her. "I'm going to miss you, Shaun... —but you'll be here when I'm back, won't you?"

"Of course I'll be here, Brittany..."

Roger, Benjamin, and Thomas told her goodbye.

. . .

She got up from the bed carefully, not wanting to wake Nigel, and treaded softly to the living room where a lined pad was lying on the coffee table. She sat in the love seat and thought of Carlton. Tears came to her eyes. As much as she had told him to move without her, she really wasn't sure she wanted him to. "I'm going to write him!" she whispered to herself and explain everything to him —make him understand!"

She reached for the lined pad with the ballpoint pen between its pages and began to write. But beyond, *Dear Carlton,* pointlessness —emptiness filled her mind, and the note pad remained blank.

Two weeks back she had returned from Daisy, and Mrs.

Hughes had called her over to talk, as they would normally do. The old woman took Shaun's right hand and turned the palm up. Mrs. Hughes gently brushed Shaun's open palm and said, "Let me read your lines, my daughter..."

"My lines," Shaun said chuckling.

"Shush!" the old woman said as she traced lines on the younger woman's palm.

"Do you see something there?"

"The boy that you left back home..." She nodded. "You will get back with him you know..."

"Mrs. Hughes... I don't know what to tell you..."

"You don't have to tell me anything... You will get back with him..." She nodded and continued. "You will get back with him..."

Shaun took a deep breath. The smell of the skunk lingered on...

"All of this and more is happening because I've given my life to the D's!" She said below her breath and took a deep breath. "No, more."

The box spring of the bed creaked.

"Shaun? —Where are you girl?

"I'm here... —outside..."

"What are you doing out there, girl? Come to bed..."

She got to her feet...

No more.

CHAPTER 19: 1996
The Montclair Story Continues

LEAVING MISS DAISY

That Monday morning when she got to the D's mansion, a bright-eyed Daisy, with Matthew on her hip let her in; immediately he reached out to Shaun.

"Wow! You can't wait to go to your second mom..."

Shaun took him. "You miss me, Matt?" she asked him.

He immediately rested his head onto her shoulders.

"He's hungry so I was just preparing something for him," Daisy said, leading off to the kitchen.

"Don't worry, Daisy, I'll do that..."

In the kitchen, Shaun deposited the toddler into his high chair and made herself busy as Daisy reorganized flowers in the bulbous blue and white vase on the dining table. "I'm trying to get used to the rest of the kids not being here," Daisy said.

When do I tell her? Shaun thought as she wiped an errant bit of baby food from the side of Matt's little mouth. *I'll tell her when I'm finished feeding Matt. I'm just going to get it over with!*

"I spoke to Brittany last night," Daisy was saying. "She didn't forget to say hi to you, Shaun..."

"That's nice..."

"You're the best nanny my kids have had, Shaun..." She was standing before the walnut colored piano on which an array of little framed pictures were arranged.

"Daisy...I have to speak to you about that..."

Daisy D turned and looked into Shaun's eyes. "About what, Shaun?"

Shaun took a deep breath. "Daisy..." She began, "this is going to be my last week here... as your nanny..."

Speechless, Daisy sat slowly in the gray, tall-backed rocker before the bank of windows with scalloped drapes offering a view to a well-manicured garden.

"Daisy... I'm sorry... but I've got to do this!"

"How could you do this to me, Shaun?" There were tears in her eyes.

"I'm sorry, Daisy... but I have to make a life of my own..."

"But the kids..."

"You'll let them know that I'm truly sorry... that I had to leave without them knowing... without telling them goodbye..."

"Why, Shaun? Why?"

"I want to have a career too... —I'm a young woman, Daisy... —you *know* I can do better that this..."

"Shaun..." Daisy said, weeping. "One person left us and then you came... and the kids have gotten so attached to you... What are they going to do, now, Shaun? —My children loves you Shaun! —What is it? Is it money? I can speak to Doctor D; we can give you another raise..."

Why can't she hear me? Shaun Stephenson though, *Why?*

"Please, Shaun..."

Shaun shook her head slowly. "I'm sorry, Daisy... I've *got* to do this... I'm sorry."

. . .

That evening she looked around the huge house in which she had been a nanny and live-in maid for two and a half years, and exulted in knowing that by the week's end, she would be saying goodbye to dirty dishes waiting to be loaded into the washer... goodbye to dropped food waiting to be wiped —scraped from the dining room's floor... goodbye to the disorder of the living room and the stairways waiting to be cleaned... goodbye to the luxurious furniture and the million and one bric-a-brac waiting to be dusted... goodbye to every strewn bit of children and adult clothing waiting to be picked up from floors, and to every assortment of odd-sized footwear waiting to be reorganized... goodbye to every hamper of sweaty clothing waiting to be lugged to the basement... goodbye to every bed waiting to be remade, and every damp towel waiting to be picked up from the bathroom floor... goodbye to every toilet bowl waiting to be cleaned... goodbye to every dirty mirror... goodbye to every corner of the vast basement waiting to be vacuumed... goodbye to the laundry room where the process of washing, drying, and folding never ends... goodbye to the preparation of someone else's dinner.

Shaun knew she would soon be saying goodbye to a life of debilitating servility... that soon she'd be saying goodbye to little Matt to whom she became attached... Matt who said his first words to her... Matt who made his first steps with her... She shrugged. There would be other nannies destined to love him. ...

She was happy because she knew that once she was free of the D's, somehow things would be better for her, even though she had only one month's rent in reserve and a few dollars left for food. What she had a limitless less supply of, however, was faith.

CHAPTER 20: 1996 • 1998
The Montclair Story Continues

FROM LIVE-IN NANNY AND MAID TO HUDSON BANK
TELLER, TO FULL SERVICE CUSTOMER REP. AT BLUE
CROSS BLUE SHIELD OF NEW JERSEY

Shaun sat over from Mrs. Hughes and pored over the classified section of the *Montclair Times* the older woman had brought her. Shaun had been sitting alone thinking of little Max... seeing his little face as he smiled and waved goodbye to her as she left Daisy's house for the last time. It hurt to leave the D's, but she had to. She had to do it for her life. It was then that she had heard a gentle knocking on the wall...

"Mrs. Hughes?"

"Yes, my daughter, what you sit down over there alone thinking? Come over man... come keep this old lady company..."

The two women sat over from each other with the remnants of goat curry and rice between them. It was now one week after Shaun had left Daisy and the need to find a new job was paramount in her mind. Nigel's salary alone would not cut it. Everything was limited, but her landlady strove to keep Shaun's spirit up.

"I know life, my girl... I know of all its ups and downs. I won't pressure you for the rent. I understand....

"All you have to do now is find something that *you* think can make you somebody in this place... If today, you don't see something in the papers that you can do, you will see something tomorrow..."

"I think there is something here... It's a bank with a vacancy for a teller..."

"Right here in Montclair?"

"Yes!" Shaun looked up; her eyes were alight with joy —with hope. "It's the Hudson United Bank..."

"Where? In Park Street?"

"Yes."

"That's not far from here. Walking distance. See? That is *your* luck..."

The next morning Shaun, dressed formally, entered the bank, and sought information. She was told that she had to see Mr. Walter Kilpatrick the branch manager. He was a stocky, pleasant guy with whom she felt at ease. She was given an application and a questionnaire that she filled ably, due to her once being a loans representative back in Guyana. After she was finished, the manager looked it over and then looked across to Shaun sitting respectful before his huge desk. He smiled. "Young woman," he said, "you've got the job. You're our newest teller. Welcome aboard."

. . .

It was a few weeks shy of one year since I'd been working for the Hudson United Bank and going to school. It was almost time to graduate. There was an ad in the Star Ledger for entry-level jobs at Blue Cross Blue Shield of New Jersey. I made three great friends while working at the bank, Sharif, Shalon, and Marjhan; we handled all transactions. It could have been said that we practically ran the bank. After we saw the ad in the newspapers, Shalon and I send our resumes to Blue Cross. It so happened that Shalon's uncle was a manger there. I knew no one at Blue Cross. We were, however, called at the same time to take the entry-level test and an interview.

We both passed the test with flying colors and were told to return a few days later to be interviewed. Shalon's uncle interviewed me. He was very kind and asked a lot about my nationality. He seemed genuinely interested in Guyana and my work background. The fact that I had worked my way from undocumented nanny and maid to being a bank teller, and now applying for a job at Blue Cross, fascinated him especially.

I then met with the recruiter. She looked at my resume and said, "Shaundal... from what I'm seeing here... you have absolutely no background in Health Insurance... but you've done well on all the test... answered these questions very well... I would say

—and must add: you do have an interesting work background... I also see that you've recently graduated from the Catherine Gibbs School... hmm... Business Administration..."

I looked at her; she looked at me.

"Well?" I said.

"Hmm..." She smiled. "You know... I can lose my job for hiring you... —but guess what? —I'll take a chance on you, Shaundal..."

"You can call me, Shaun, please..."

"Okay, Shaun," she said. "You'll hear from us in a few days."

I thanked her, told her how grateful I was, and promised to do my best to learn all there is about my job.

. . .

Early one morning the phone at the bank rang. It was someone from Blue Cross asking to speak to me. When I answered the phone it was the recruiter. "Hi, Shaun." she said. "I'd like to make you an offer to work for Blue Cross as a full Service Customer Rep... How does that sound?"

It took all I had to contain my excitement, and told her I needed to give the bank two weeks notice —which was understood.

I was destined to begin working with Horizon Blue Cross Blue Shield of New Jersey in December, and would graduate from Katherine Gibbs the following month.

The bank didn't want to lose me, however; they proposed to raise my salary, but the offer I had from Blue Cross was captivating. Along with that, I was determined to face a new challenge: to find a place in the Health Insurance Industry.

. . .

I had learned to drive and bought my first car: a brand new Hyundai Accent. The interesting thing was, I didn't know how to get from Montclair to Newark where the Blue Cross office was. So Nigel took me there on a dry run. Yet, I was apprehensive about driving there by myself on the day of the orientation, since Nigel would be at work. *Would I remember the way?*

"Don't worry, Shaun," Shalon said. "We'll go together; I'll drive ahead of you and you'll follow. Okay?"

That sounded great to me, but things did not work out as planned and I ended up driving to Newark all alone. I was nervous, a bit unsure, but I calmed myself and made the trip. I ended up being half an hour late for the orientation and was profusely apologetic on entering the room. I told them all about it being my first time driving from Montclair to Newark and most, it seemed, understood. "Don't worry about it, Shaun," the recruiter said. "Actually we've just started. Just find a seat, take a breath, and settle in."

After orientation and training ended, those of us moving on were placed into teams. What I found overwhelming was the number of employees I was cast amongst. Back in Guyana, the branch of the national bank where I worked, there were no more forty people and that included a pair of security guards. At the Hudson United Bank, there were about six of us. And here I was a Blue Cross surrounded by two thousand plus employees of differing, nationalities, ages, and personalities. But out of it, there was one very matured woman I could have related with quite easily: Andrea Panico, and she and I became good friends. We looked out for each other and did a lot of Blue Cross projects together. She was White and of Grecian heritage; I was Black and of African heritage. But it did not matter; we bonded as two women who could have spoken to each other about almost anything.

That year, there was a special administrative account that was so problematic; many feared the Company was going to lose it. There was apparently a ton of work to be done to make it right. Morale was low on the team handling this account.

"Can't we help them fix whatever account it is?" I asked my supervisor.

She shrugged. "You want to help them?"

"I wouldn't mind... —as I see it, the more I'm involved in, the more I learn... I can do it on overtime..."

"Okay, Shaun..." My supervisor said. "It's your funeral. Go up to the fifth floor and ask for Mrs. Bindhu Lurkhur. Just tell her that you're there to help with the Account... She'll tell you what you can do."

"Okay," I said, all bright-eyed and busy-tailed.

. . .

When I first met Bindhu Lurkhur she was an Assistant Team Leader. I remember I said, "Hello, are you Bindhu?"

"Yes, I am," she answered and I picked up her Trinidadian accent.

"I'm Shaun," I said. "And I came up to help... —in any way that I can..."

"Where are you from, Shaun? —I hear an accent..." she said cheerily.

"I'm from Guyana," I said, "and you're Trinidadian."

And we were laughing together.

"Okay..." Bindhu said.

She gave me a stack of old files, and told me that they were very backlogged — that I can do whatever can, to put them in order. As I delved deeper into them, I soon realized that much of the stuff on the system needed to be deleted. There were claims that needed to be rekeyed, and there were other claims that needed to be broken down into manageable details.

"It's a lot to do, Shaun... I know."

"Don't worry...I can handle it, Bindhu..."

When I told her what I thought would have been the best approach to move the work along, she was impressed.

Bindhu and I gradually bonded, and she began to show me the in and outs of the system —short cuts and little tricks that helped moved things along. That was when I said to myself: *I need to leave my current team and join Bindhu's team so I can really learn —so that I would have that chance to excel in the company.* Fortunately for me it was a time when individuals were leaving the team Bindhu managed because they could not handle the stress and backlog. Bindhu approached me one day and asked if I would like to work on with her? I didn't hesitate. I said yes. Soon after, she was promoted to Team Leader.

Over the years Bindhu and I got closer. Her husband, children and her family got to know and like me. I would spend weekends at Bindhu's house helping Sam, her husband, cook. We used to hang out at her back yard in Tiffany Blvd Newark. We did grocery shopping and took trips together.

Bindhu Lurkhur became like the elder sister I never had.

· · ·

BASCOM: And through these years, what's happening with you and Carlton?

SHAUN: Carlton is still communicating with me. (*Shakes her head.*) And still doesn't know I'm married... I'm telling him to move on with his life... (*Shook her head.*) But he continues to call —continues to write me —giving me updates on the house he was rebuilding...

BASCOM: But you never came out and told him to stop communicating with you —that you didn't want to hear from him.

SHAUN: (*Shakes her head.*) I couldn't do something like that... (*Sighs.*) Whether I liked it or not, I was connected to Carlton... still cared about Carlton... cared about his mother Joyce and how much we went through together...

BASCOM: So, at *this* point what's happening between you Nigel?

SHAUN: At this point in time, we have already left Mrs. Hughes place in Chestnut and are in a much larger apartment in Fullerton Street —not far from Chestnut... (*Shakes her head.*) And this turns out to be a very turbulent year for me emotionally...

BASCOM: In what way?

SHAUN: Well... things fell apart between Nigel and myself... He started doing things I couldn't deal with, and then *I* began doing things *he* couldn't deal with —(*Shrugs.*) The marriage began to fall apart... So one night Carlton calls... and I tell him I want to see him, and we agree to meet in Trinidad...

BASCOM: You wanted to come clean...

CHAPTER 21: 1998
Trinidad & Tobago

COMING CLEAN

These two islands, hugging the coast of Venezuela, are excellent getaways for travelers who shun the well-trodden tourist track and who like their vacations more spontaneous than planned. Trinidad, at one thousand eight hundred and sixty four square miles, is by far the larger and worldlier of the two; indeed 'worldly' takes on a new meaning here for nowhere on earth perhaps is there a place that can more justly call itself a melting pot. Trinidad's astonishing ethnic mix —African, Asian, East Indian, European, South American, and Middle Eastern—has produced a splendidly harmonious patchwork of cultural expression. ...

There was a carnival in her chest as the jet decelerated on the runway at the Piarco International Airport, and taxied in. Soon it would come to a stop; soon the motorized stairways would be in place... soon the disembarkation. She peered from her window seat to the sprawling, colorful terminal building and knew that Carlton the man whom had been in her life since she was thirteen waited. An air valve hissing above her seat helped her to be calm as she took her carry-on bag from the rack, and then she was moving with the others passengers for the door where the Portuguese Captain bade everyone goodbye with his Trinidadian accent.

Shaun closed her eyes.

What would Doods do when he sees me? Will he hug me? I know I will hug him... And when we get settled, how do I tell him about all that had passed back through five years since I last saw him? Will he hate me for the deception —my pretence —my lies —the way I had been making him a fool?

She exited the aircraft into a sun-drenched Caribbean zephyr. On the tarmac the Black and Indian workers were getting the suitcases out of the aircraft's belly. She heard their carefree banter and her joy to be back in familiar surroundings assuaged her anxiety for a moment. It was as though she was home in Guyana fifty minutes away.

She entered the terminal building and started towards the Customs & Immigration checkpoint.

What would Doods look like after five years?

They hadn't exchanged a lot of photographs.

Having passed through Customs & Immigration she got her luggage and headed for the arrivals lounge where pan music emanated. She looked around for him... and then she spotted Carlton through a gap in the milling carnival of people in the arrivals area. He smiled in that shy, mischievous way she remembered.

Should I hug him first?

But even as her mind popped questioned her arms were open and reaching out to him as he reached out for her. They hugged wordlessly amidst the piped music and the hubbub of greetings.

. . .

She felt him looking at her as the taxi took them to the motel room that he had rented in Port of Spain. "What?" she said.

"I'm looking at your hair..."

It was braided ala Rastafarian. "You like it?"

He laughed and nervously fingered a lock. "You're a dread, now..."

"Not really... just a style..."

"Which horse you killed to get all this, hair, girl?"

She laughed, sighed covertly and reached for his hand.

"This is the first time you coming to Trinidad, Miss?" the taxi driver said over his shoulder, then concluded before Shaun could have answered. "Very different from America, eh?"

"I was here before," Shaun said.

"Once you get a taste of T.T... you're bound to come again, my friend."

At last they reached the motel. It was not what she had expected. It was a shabby little facility not far from a cricket ground. The room he had gotten for them, however, wasn't that bad. It was clean... the bed looked comfortable.

He came in with the last suitcase and she was sitting on the side of the bed. He rested the luggage down and sat next to her.

"Babes, if you're tired from the flight you can rest a bit," he said. "I'm going to order something for you..." He started to his feet.

"No! No, Doods..." She restrained him gently. "I'm not hungry. Tonight we can go for a walk and get something to eat..." She turned and lay back on the bed. "Come...lie with me."

He lay next to her as if he were her brother. For a while they lay wordlessly, her eyes closed; his fixed to the ceiling with the slowly revolving fan.

"Babes..." he said at last.

"Sssh! ... I know there's so much to talk about, Doods...but not now... not now..."

"Okay..." he whispered.

"Just hold me, Doods..."

And he did; and she felt him; and she was unable to stem her tears.

· · ·

SHAUN: There was so much burning on my heart to get out... (*Shakes her head.*) And the key thing I had to tell him about was the marriage. (*Shakes her head.*) He didn't know at the time...

BASCOM: So explaining things to him was your main focus...

SHAUN: (*Nods.*) But initially neither of us seemed able to start talking about those years between us... (*Shrugs.*) So we talked instead about what's going on back in Guyana... going on at home back the village... who married who... who's had babies and how old they are... —because I've been gone five years —there was a whole new generation to go back to... So those things came up —the yard... the garden... how things were going with the business —Carlton had his own graphic arts business at the time. So we small-talked about all that stuff... the house at Best road that he had actually started having rebuilt... So (*She sighs.*) that's the stuff we talked about initially. I didn't get into talking about the marriage to Nigel until that night when we went out to get something to eat...

. . .

On their way back from the restaurant, they walked hand in hand along the street took them past Kensington Oval. To her the night was balmy. She took a deep breath. It was a goodnight for getting things off one's chest.

After he closed and locked the door behind him, she looked up at him as she slipped off her shoes.

"We're going to talk?" he said.

Shaun nodded. He sat next to her and put an arm around her shoulder. She sighed and leaned into him.

"Let's lie down, Babes," he said.

"You want to start?" She asked.

"There's so much I have to ask you... so much I didn't understand... and still don't..."

"What is it you want to know?"

"I've heard so many things about you..." He shook his head. "And missing you made those things hard to take, Babes..."

"I'm sorry, Doods," She sighed. "If you heard that I was married... well that's true... I *am* married —but it's over, actually... I'm going to get a divorce soon..."

Carlton got up and went to the sole window of the room. Silhouetted in the frame of light through the blinds she saw his huge intake of breath.

She sat up. "You have to hear me out, Doods... —I know it's hard... but you have to hear me out..."

"Okay..." He turned and sat next to her. She took his hand and sensed a slight tremor. She squeezed it.

"I heard this," he said. "But I was adamant that I was *not* going to take anybody's word for it. You never told me that... I told them it wasn't true —that if there was a man you were living with... a man whom you married, you would have told me..." He shook his head. "I didn't believe them!"

She sighed. "It was true, Carlton..." She looked into his hurt eyes. "You want to hear about it?"

He said nothing.

"I think I need to let you know why whatever took place, took place..."

"I understand," he said, his voice very low. "There was no other easy way you could have stayed... and gotten a green card..." He shook his head. "But why you kept so many things from me, Shaun?" Agitation entered his voice: "This is what I can't understand!" He took a deep, stabilizing voice, and then said, his tone conciliatory: "It's okay... you came back to me." He shook his head as if in some sort of inner torment and continued. "You know what, Babes? ... I blame myself! Yes... I have to blame myself for you leaving in the first place... for you having to end up over in America going through what you had to go through..."

"No, Doods... you don't have to blame yourself for anything... Let me tell you everything..."

"I DON'T WANT TO HEAR EVERYTHING! ...I *don't* want to hear everything..." He took a deep breath. "And you're still married."

"Yes, but as I told you, I'll be divorced soon."

He said nothing for a while,

Is this a mistake?

Was I wrong to come?

Will this work out for us?

Has too much gone on in my life that Carlton cannot accept —refuses to accept?

She felt his arms around her once more. "It's okay, Babes... You are here for me... We're all we've got... we're all *we've* got..."

"I'm sorry, Doods..."

"It's I who am sorry, Babes... if I were more of a man for you in the first place you wouldn't have left... It's *I* who am sorry..."

Five days later she boarded her return flight for *JFK*. As she sat back in her seat waiting for the plane to take off, she recalled the night. She and Carlton had just come in from a quiet walk in the shadows of the Oval.

"Babes," he said. "I have something for you, but you have to close your eyes."

"What?" she asked giggling.

"Close your eyes first, Babes...."

She did and he placed something gently in her right hand, and closed the palm over it.

"Okay... you can look now..."

It was a beautiful little jewel box, and it in was an engagement ring.

Shaun fitted herself a bit more snugly in her window seat, and in her mind she knew that it would only be a matter of time when she would return to Guyana and Carlton and fulfill the promise she had made... of being his wife.

CHAPTER 22: 2007
Leaving Oklahoma

We checked out of the Best Western and boarded the shuttle that was waiting to take us to the Will Rogers Airport. Check in time was at 10: 00 AM flight. The flight was scheduled to leave at 12:00 Noon. When we got there, however, we found that no checking-in was being done.

What's going on?

Then at about 11:45 A.M. an announcement was made: The plane scheduled to fly us out of Oklahoma was experiencing mechanical problems and as such, the flight was cancelled until sometime on Monday afternoon the earliest. The reaction to this news surprised me: No one swore; no one sighed; no one openly complained. We just stood... sat... and waited. And in waiting I made the acquaintance of a Pre-paid Legal Executive from Georgia, Mr. Fred Curling whom I had never been introduced to formally. I had, however, said hello to him in passing a few days earlier.

"So what we going to do, Shaun?" Mom asked.

"You know what?" I said. "Let me go and speak to this flight attendant..."

I went over to the counter and engaged a representative of our airline. She told me that a good alternative would be to get to Texas and catch a flight out to Philadelphia.

"That's a great idea..." I said.

"Well then," she said consulting her computer. "Let's see what's available..." She tapped a few keys... "I'm seeing... that there's a flight out of Texas and it has... one seat! You are in luck!"

"I'm sorry," I said, "but it's three of us —myself, my mom and my aunt..."

She laughed lightly. "One seat definitely would not do —but let's not lose hope..." She began to tap at her keyboard once more.

Just then Fred Curling joined me at the counter. "Excuse me my dear," he said, "but while you're at it, can you please see if there's a connecting flight from Texas to Georgia..."

"Okay, sir..." She continued to tap at her keyboard, and then her face lit up. "Here we go... You're both in luck... there is a flight leaving Texas for Pennsylvania with three seats..." Then she turned to Fred, "If you're going to Georgia you too are in luck. There's a plane leaving Texas for that location too. That leaves, however, at 9:00 P.M...."

"I'll take it..."

By now my mom who had made friends with Sharon an associate from California piped in, "What about from Texas to California, Miss?"

And would you know it, there was also a flight leaving at 10:00 P.M. for California. All we had to work out was how we were going to get from Oklahoma to Texas.

"We simply rent something that can take us all," Fred said with an authority I guess he was used to." He turned once more to the attendant. "How long a drive might that be?"

"I'd say approximately four hours..."

"We can share the driving, Fred." I said

"So let's do it, Shaun."

Fred headed to Enterprise Rent-A-Car, while I got about retrieving our suitcases from baggage claim. He came back with a minivan; we loaded our stuff, and got in.

"Is this the first time you're here, Shaun?" he said.

"Actually, yes..."

"I've been here a couple of times, so... as I have some experience driving on the West Coast..." He smiled and got into the driver's seat. "So I'll do the driving duties, okay?"

And we were on our way to Texas.

Fred and I got to know each other better. He was from Jamaican and had been in the United States for over thirty years. He had a wife and three children, and one of his business partner and best friend was from Guyana. So we chatted about Guyana for a while.

At last we got into Texas. The landscape fascinated me. I wished I had a camera. Most of us were oohing and aahing at the beauty of the trees and mountains along the highway. We passed farms with lots of cows and horses, and the roads were wide and traffic was moderate. We even came upon an accident that slowed the traffic. Then there were towns we passed with strip malls with similar stores as on the East Coast.

. . .

At last signs for the Dallas Airport started showing up along the route. I could not believe it. It took us less than three hours even though we were told four. Mom and Aunt Bridget had a great time with their newfound friend Sharon who, my aunt thought looked just like her daughter-in-law. The three women bonded well on our road trip.

Fred pointed. "The entrance to the airport's coming up," he said.

Soon after, we pulled up at the airport, disembarked, got our stuff out.

Then it was a time for separation. We all exchanged phone numbers, hugs, goodbyes, and headed for separate buses to take us the terminal where we were destined to board our separate planes back to our respective states.

It was a memorable experience.

CHAPTER 23: 1998
The Montclair Story Continues

RESTARTING FROM THE BOTTOM: THE MOVE TO
DANNY'S BASEMENT

Shaun stared out of the window of her Fullerton Street apartment. A Verizon van waited at the Chestnut Street intersection, turn-lights blinking. At last it swung slowly into her street. Shaun looked up at the tree outside her window at its browning leaves soon to fall. *When I came it was just like this*, she thought and smiled in remembering her bafflement about the trees... *"Aunt Claudette... why are the leaves falling? —Are the trees dying?"*

She closed her eyes, took a deep breath, and thought of Nigel... thought of Carlton... thought of her life. *Where am I going?* Now she was familiar with the seasonal changes of nature and of life. It was fall and her fortunes had indeed been as variable as the colors of the autumn leaves in her unfocused gaze.

She heard a door close in the apartment above her and recalled the fight she and Nigel had after she returned from the Twin Island. Soon after, they separated, and she filed for a divorce. The kettle was whistling from the kitchen. Shaun opened her eyes and wended her way through the living room's furniture she and Nigel had bought and turned the stove off. In the wake of the faded whistling the silence in the apartment crept close and hemmed her in. Nigel was gone. The landlord had rented him another apartment over in East Orange.

She sipped tea and contemplated her situation. She knew that, alone, she wouldn't be able to continue paying the rent on the salary she was making. She had to move to an apartment she could afford. She sighed. *Where can I go? Maybe I can call the Haitian guy... Danny. Would he hold it against me that we had broken that first lease with him?* She sighed and urged herself: *Call him, Shaun! You're no stranger to Danny!*

Through the years he had been her source for immigrant-related information. But how would he react to her wanting to rent space from him again, she wasn't sure. *I'll call him. What is there to loose?*

She retraced her steps to the loveseat where she had deposited her workbag, and took out her planner with Danny's number. She called him and he was happy to hear from her. She asked him about an apartment for herself. He told her that the only space he could have thought of was his basement, but that it needed a lot of work to make it livable.

"So," she said. "What if I am willing to invest some money to fix it up?"

"That sounds like something we can do, yes. Then why not come around and see it and we'll take it from there?"

.   .   .

I stopped by to see the basement one afternoon after work, and yes, there was much work to be done. He wanted four hundred dollars per month in rent but agreed to drop it to just three hundred and fifty since I was going to do the renovations to make it livable. We shook on that and I went looking for carpets and other amenities. It cost quite a bit to put Danny's basement in order, but with the help of a good friend who was into construction it was done within one week.

So I broke the lease with my Fullerton Street landlord, lost the initial deposit, and moved into Danny's basement. And moving didn't cost me a dime since another good friend of mine who owned a little caravan helped out.

While all this was going on, I was very worried about the fact that I had filed for a divorce from Nigel. I knew that so doing was a very big risk, since my eligibility for Permanent Residency status was hinged on being married to him. But I just could not stay in the marriage any longer. Once my divorce came through, my hope of remaining legally in America was going to be in jeopardy. I prayed about it. This was the kind of trepidation that moved with me to Danny's basement where I knew I had to start life in America all over again and literally from the bottom.

I did my best to make my humble basement apartment comfortable, but it took some getting used to. What got me was that it was always dark down there... always night down there, and the lights had to be on continually. Weren't it for the clock on my bed stand and the one on the wall closest to the furnace room, I never could have known what time of day it was. I told myself that I was going to get used to it, but I never did. At heart I was a child of open air and light, and knew that my sojourn in Danny's basement was not going to be long.

. . .

One evening Danny came down to check the boiler, and I was in. "Shaun," he said to me. "You ever heard of something —a company named Pre-Paid Legal Services?"

"No," I said. "What is it about?"

"It's something," he said, "that you can pay just a little money for per month and access an attorney for any situation you might find yourself in..."

"In other words, if I need a lawyer I wouldn't have to rob a bank to pay them?"

He laughed. "No. Once you subscribe to this service, you'll be able to call a lawyer and get consultations, and even if there is a cost, you will get a special cut cost..."

"Interesting... —so how much money would I have to pay per month to this thing?"

"The same amount I pay —nine dollars and ninety-five cents... that's why I got it, and I think it can help you..."

"Wow..."

"I can sign you up if you're interested..."

I completed an application without hesitation, wrote a check and became a Pre-Paid Legal member. It turned out to be a very sensible nine dollars and ninety-nine cents per month invest-ment I ever made, since soon after it turned out that I needed to use the service for my complex immigration process when I was planning to return home in December. The Pre-Paid legal lawyers guided me and advised me through the entire process without me incurring thousands of dollars in attorney fees.

CHAPTER 24: 1998

The Montclair Story Continues

TO GUYANA, SOUTH AMERICA, AND BACK

I could hardly believe that I had booked a flight and was packed and ready to return home on a visit to Guyana after five years. I had made a promise to myself that I would have become a Permanent Resident before my fifth year in America, and I had done it in a little under four. Now I could have traveled. It was an achievement.

My flight home was going to be a surprise too, since only Carlton knew I was coming and had promised to keep it a secret.

That night before I flew out, I sat in Danny's basement with a pair of bulging suitcases, overweight with enough gifts for everyone, and I was happy. In my mind I anticipated that surging of joy to finally see my family and friends again... to see Carlton's nieces and nephews. I knew I was headed to face a whole new generation of children, some five years of age and younger —most of whom I had seen only in pictures.

The next day I checked in for my BWIA flight and my suitcases, as I anticipated, were overweight. But I guess because I was early, I was checked out without a problem.

I got to my seat and settled in for a flight that was destined to be a little less than seven hours due to the scheduled stopover in Trinidad en-route to Guyana. There was a knot of butterflies in my stomach as I waited for the plane to lift off. And on the threshold of landing back in Guyana I thought of many things...

How much has Guyana changed? Is the bridge still operating? Has the ferry service between Georgetown City and Vreeden-Hoop improved? What about Phoenix Park where I grew with my grandparents? What about Crane Scheme where my mother lived? What about Best Village where Carlton and his mother Joyce lived?

When the plane lifted off, I was thinking about the new house being built where the old house stood. Carlton told me that roof as—well as all the walls—was up, and that they were already living in it. I smiled to myself. It was Christmas, so there would be much ado about decorating.

The pilot was telling us about cruising speed and stuff like that, but in my mind I was reliving a Guyanese Christmas Eve night —that last minute hustle and bustle to be ready for Christmas morning...

In my mind I could have smelled pepper pot, black cake, and freshly baked bread. Christmas in Guyana is nothing like America. In Guyana it is all about family and sharing.

I settled back in my seat, closed my eyes, and imagined a scene of excitement when the news got around the village, that 'Battery's daughter' had returned. I knew most would be looking for 'something' once they knew I was home.

After less that than an hour in Trinidad, the plane finally landed at Timehri International Airport, in Guyana, South America.

I got though immigration without a hassle, and emerged into tropical sunlight with my suitcases. When I saw the amount of children begging it broke my heart. Soon after, however, I walked into Carlton's open arms. Hugs and kisses. We had just been together a few months ago in Trinidad, but this was home and it felt good to be back after such a long time.

He had his own car so we didn't need a taxi. On the way home, he told me stories of returning Guyanese who met with unfortunate events en route from the airport.

"Doods," I said. "I think I'm safe with you in this car, okay? Spare me those stories, and let me enjoy looking at my country...."

What stood out was the amount of new and renovated houses along the East Bank. Then, of course there were those things that seem timeless —like the vendors on the roadside with stands of bananas, papaya, sorrel, oranges, and lots and lots of pineapples...

We came upon the Demerara Harbor Bridge and it was retracted for river traffic, so we waited in the snaking line of cars to cross over the Demerara River and home. I remembered this from years ago.

Carlton and I got out of the car. He bought me cane juice while we waited. Then the bridge came back together again, the cars began to move, and we were on our way home.

I had heard that my old school, West Demerara Secondary High, burnt down and was rebuilt. I was eager to see it as we swung into Pouderoyen and past the venerable Malgre Tout Catholic Church, the old Starlite Cinema, the rustic sawmill... Bob's Funeral Parlor, Middle Street, the koker... and then I saw the new school building and it seemed so strange to me. Surreal.

At last we made a left turn onto Latchmansingh highway and entered New Road Village that led to Crane Scheme. There were lots of other changes; it took me awhile to place where things used to be. Shortly after, we were on the road that led to the Best Hospital. Carlton made a left onto Best Road where they lived, and the cemetery where my grandma was buried was over on the right.

I thought of the wristwatch decorated with little diamonds that I had sent after she died, and said a little prayer in my mind for her. I found myself remembering Grandma who took care of me as a baby and whom I had grown up with... my grandma whom I loved as my mother. *Sorry I could not attend your funeral, Grandma,* I thought, and the memories welled up in me. I was her first grand-child and she loved me. Carlton glanced over at me.

"You okay, Babes?"

"Only passing memories..." I told him. "

He reached over and squeezed my hand. "Of your grand-mother... I know... If you get time before you go back, maybe you can visit her tomb..."

"Maybe..."

At last we pulled into the driveway and Joyce my mother-in-law was on the veranda. I came out of the car, she recognized me and screamed. The surprise was complete.

"BABES! —OH MY GOD YOU COME HOME!"

Carlton was laughing, and before you knew it everyone was running, excitedly, over into my mother-in-law's yard to hug and welcome me back to sunshine and neighborly love. As Joyce hugged me she was laughing and crying and reluctant to share me with the neighbors. Soon Carlton's nieces and nephews who had been amidst the fruit tress in the backyard were about me jumping up and down like Massai warriors.

"Everybody will get a chance to talk to, Babes," Carlton said, laughing. "She's had a long flight. Let her get a chance to go in the house and sit down.

I was truly overwhelmed about my reception and I was also overwhelmed with the house. It was coming together beautifully. Carlton did an awesome job with the design. It was stylish and very contemporary. Joyce was going to be very comfortable and proud.

By nightfall the house was filled with family, friends, and old acquaintances. I shared out stuff that I had brought and everyone seemed happy. Many who came by reminisced about life before I left them, and about life after I left them. Some spoke about what life was destined to be after I returned. Of course they wanted to know about my life in America, and I shared much of the sweet but not so much of the bitter. It was morning when Carlton and me finally said good night to our guests and went to bed. I hardly slept that night.

When the morning broke, the fresh ocean breeze came though the wide-open shutters, and with it, the smell of freshly baked bread and cocoa... and I heard Carlton's mom preparing breakfast as she sang a hymn of joy unspeakable. I lay still and quiet by Carlton's side. I did not want to wake him.

On a screen in my mind so many sweet days of our growing up together replayed. I covertly took a deep breath of satisfaction. I could not help recalling those days back in New Jersey when it dawned on me that I could not have kept so many promises I had made... I could not help recalling those days back in New Jersey when I wanted to come home but could not...

My tears came without warning and I allowed it to flow... and it flowed from deep within because of gratitude, and peace... because I had made it back home... because Carlton and I still had a chance for a life together. We had come a long way and I was about to enjoy a week with the man I guess I was connected to, for better, for bitter, for worse...

I endeavored to enjoy my week home before heading back

to the U.S. to continue the process of moving forward with my dreams for my family and having them all join me.

It was a deeply satisfying week. Best of all were the many courses of home cooked meals that I missed. Simple local foods like Eddo Callaloo and rice with dhal, coconut choka, shrimps and bush fish, constituted a royal treat for me. I was so back in my indigenous elements I tried eating with my hands as I did years back as a child. My family laughed to see me try, with my Americanized fingers.

I visited my mom and dad for a little while. Things were well with them. Between my mom and me... my dad and me however, there was a lot a healing still to happen.

Leaving was not easy. Carlton said I took a piece of him every time I left. It was hard for my mother-in-law as well.

My flight was scheduled to leave Guyana at noon. I hugged my mother-in-law, kissed each of the kids, and reluctantly entered Carlton's car. We headed to the Airport with enough time to spare, and along the way there wasn't much said in words.

I was destined to return that Christmas, one year later.

.   .   .

I came back to New Jersey with new aspirations. My divorce was final, and even though that was a relief, there was still the impending interview with the INS at which I had to be present with Nigel.

A few months after I returned from Guyana, the letter for my permanent residence interview came and I called Nigel. I said to him, "Nigel... I got the letter from the INS, for us to go in for that interview..."

"Okay..."

"Okay?"

"Okay, I'll come with you... I'll come with you and say and do whatever is needed to make sure that you get your papers, Shaun..."

I was so grateful.

My ex-husband came with to the immigration interview and we sat with other couples. Eventually we were called in. Nigel and I sat before the immigration officer and the interview began.

I began fielding her questions and it didn't sit well with the immigration officer. "Misses Hunte, if you please, I'd prefer, Nigel, your husband to answer any question that I direct to him."

I guess I had been fielding all of the questions because I knew that we were already divorced and only pretending to be still married. I guess I wasn't confident that Nigel could have pulled it off.

"Are you and Shaundal here still married?"

"Yes, we are!"

She asked him if we own a home or if we rented... where he worked... if he and I filed taxes jointly... In the end, Nigel's answers were apparently satisfactory, and that was when he said to her, "Madam, Shaun is my wife... and I want her to have her papers."

In the end our case was approved and I was granted Permanent Resident status.

When we got outside I sighed in relief, and I thanked Nigel... I will be forever grateful for him standing by me even though we had been divorced.

CHAPTER 25: 2007
Texas to Philadelphia

We boarded our plane from Texas at 9: P.M. that Sunday night and I soon fell asleep —something I could never have done in an aircraft. It all changed after September 11th, 2006. I had found my inner truth and my inner truth was discovering my 'I AM' self, and in my spiritual purpose I knew that there was nothing to fear —the least death.

I awoke after we had landed at Philadelphia's International Airport. It was now Monday and my mind was as fresh as the morning wind. After we claimed our baggage, my mom, aunt, and myself waited on the shuttle that would take us over the Walt Whitman Bridge to New Jersey, and on to my home in Mantua.

There was a lot going on in my head. I was fired up from the Convention and was eager to apply what I had learnt. In my mind I was making a list —who to call —what appointments I had to make. I was thinking of my team —about getting them together for a meeting in order to share all of the new information I had gathered from Oklahoma. I was also thinking of myself between my Blue Cross Blue Shield job that paid the mortgage and kept the lights, and an overwhelming commitment to my Pre-Paid Legal Services endeavors.

I took out a note pad and began to map out a plan for the coming days. I even had an appointment scheduled for 9: A.M. on the very morning we waited for the shuttle bus. It was about 1: A.M. I presumed that we'd get home by 2:30 A.M. I knew that if I needed to keep an appointment at daybreak, there wouldn't be much time to rest, so I was glad that I had slept the entire flight from Texas more or less.

As we waited on the shuttle I mapped out my game plan: per-sonal goals —team goals —daily activities and commitments. The one thing that kept getting in the way of my plans was my job. I could not give fourteen-hour days to my regular job if I wanted this business to work. Granted: I had requested to be part-time, was granted part-time, but the work got no less.

My PPLSI commitment and commitments to my other entre-preneurial interests were often coming into conflict with my Blue Cross job. Because of it, I found myself having to meet with clients during my lunch break. In order to find time, I found myself get-ting up and signing onto the Blue Cross Blue Shield system at 5: A.M. and working until 2: P.M. —nine straight hours with no over time compensation. That was a sacrifice I had to make to keep the lights on —to keep my home running. And it became harder because I had developed a reputation as that go-to person at Blue Cross. I was seen as trainer and troubleshooter for all the teams I associated with. I seemed always deluged by emails requesting my assistance in one thing or the other. Even working part time wasn't allowing me the time I needed for my work as a PPLSI Independent Associate, and I made the decision. I was going to leave the health insurance company altogether.

Because Carlton had started his own business back in Guyana, I thought he would have been the first to understand what a full commitment to Pre-Paid Legal Services would mean for me... —for him —and for our relatives.

Eventually we boarded the shuttle.

When I get home, I thought to myself. *I'm going to tell him! I'm going to say to him: "I'm going to leave my Blue Cross job, Doods..."*

I told myself that I was going to make him understand how serious I was about making it as a successful Pre-paid Legal Associate.

I told myself that he *would* understand and support my decision.

CHAPTER 26: 1999

East Orange, New Jersey

ON BECOMING A PRE-PAID LEGAL SERVICES ASSOCIATE

Although still a small percentage of total residents, Orange and East Orange have the largest concentrations of Guyanese Americans in the country. In the 2000 Census, 2.5% of East Orange residents identified as being of Guyanese ancestry. While Queens and Brooklyn had larger populations in terms of raw numbers, Orange (with 2.9%) and East Orange had the highest percentage of people of Guyanese ancestry as a portion of the total population of all places in the United States with at least 1,000 people identifying their ancestry.

By now I was in East Orange, renting a two-bedroom attic of a vast house owned by the Hendersons, a wonderful couple. For a top story, it was very spacious with an enormous master bedroom. There was one bath, a living room, an eat-in kitchen, two walk-in closets and three large spaces for storage.

By then, however, I had become jaded about renting. I was now thinking that I wanted to own my own house. And so, ignorant of the business of credit scores as it related directly to the acquisition of real estate in America, I drove back to Montclair and began to look for a property to buy. I drove around the City until I saw a sign that said, 'For Sale By Owner' and stopped to enquire.

The owner of the house turned out to be one Susanne Salaam, a mortgage company representative who was selling her house. She invited me in and complimented me on wanting to own my own place. I think we connected right away, and she began showing me around her home.

When we got to the master bedroom there was a wedding dress on a mannequin. "That's Pretty," I said. "Are you getting married?"

She laughed. "That's my wedding dress from a few years ago, girl..." She delicately fingered the lace on a sleeve.

"I'll be getting married soon..." I said and didn't know why. There was something about Suzanne that made me want to open up to her —to speak to her, woman to woman, even though we had met less than half an hour ago.

"Wow! —Congratulations!"

"Thank you..."

"I can give this dress to you if you want..."

"Mrs. Salaam..."

"Why don't you try it on?"

"You're sure?"

"Come on, girl..."

I tried it on and it was a tad too big.

"It looks a little large on you..."

"And I wouldn't want to do alterations on it... it's too beautiful..."

"Okay," she said as I slipped my own clothes on. "Let me continue to show you the house."

"Okay..."

"So have you begun talking to any bank from which you can apply for a mortgage?"

"Really, Suzanne, all I know is that I need to get a place of my own. I've been renting here and there..."

So we spoke about the ins and outs of buying a house in America, and then she said to me, "Wouldn't you like to own your own business, Shaun? —To be your own boss one day?"

I giggled, surprised at the question, taken aback by the sincerity in her voice. "Who wouldn't, Susanne?"

"Have you ever heard of Pre-Paid Legal Services Incorporated?"

"Yes, I have!" I said. "I'm actually a member. My old landlord signed me up, and I think it's something very convenient. It saved me a ton of money!"

"Do you know that your Landlord actually made money when he signed you up and that if he can sign up a lot of other people like yourself he can stand to make a lot of money?"

"Really..."

She nodded. "It's a business, Shaun. You can make money telling people about it and signing them up..."

"I had no idea..."

"If you become an associate it would be your business. And what you'll be doing is going out to meet people —groups of people and talking to them —doing presentations on how Pre-Paid Legal can make their lives easier..." She shrugged. "And make money signing up those interested."

"How can I get involved?"

"Listen, I have an presentation coming up..."

"Where?"

"Right here —a home presentation. I'm inviting you and whichever friends you want to bring along to it..."

"Okay... I can do that, and I can bring someone along..." I told her.

I was excited and wanted to know more about Pre-Paid Legal. So after I left Suzanne Salaam's home, I called my Trinidadian friend Bindhu with whom I worked at Blue Cross Blue Shield. I told her about Suzanne, Pre-paid legal Services, the presentation Suzanne was going to have, and Bindhu agreed to come with me.

We attended the meeting and I watched and listened keenly as Suzanne salaam did a presentation... and as I sat there something said to me, *Shaun... you can do this! This is something that you can do! You can speak well! You are sincere! There is something about you that people trust! Shaun, you too can do this! You too can become a Pre-Paid Legal Associate!*

I spoke to Suzanne afterwards. The cost to get started was two hundred and forty-nine dollars. All the money I had at that point was just my rent that was due. But becoming a Pre-Paid Legal associate was important enough gamble with my rent. I cast caution to the wind, took the sign-up fee from the due rent and signed up with Suzanne. I told myself that the Hendersons would understand and give me a break with the rent. They did. Bindhu also joined and became my first recruit.

Suzanne Salaam and I became very close friends. She taught me the basic ins and outs of the Pre-paid Legal business and something deep within me signaled my future.

CHAPTER 27: 2007

Mantua, New Jersey

Mantua Township is located in the center of Gloucester County, just South of the County Seat of Woodbury. It is 19.89 square miles bounded by Greenwich and West Deptford Townships to the North; the Borough of Wenonah, Deptford and Washington Townships to the East; the Borough of Pitman and part of Glassboro Borough to the South; Harrison Township to the Southwest and East Greenwich Township to the West. It is situated on an elevated bluff overlooking Mantua Creek, from which the township derives its name.

JUNE. Pre-Paid Legal Director Shaun Stephenson pulled into her driveway and parked facing the house she had bought two years ago. She breathed evenly, calmly as she gazed past the deck Carlton her husband had renovated. A year or so back he might have been coming out to see if she needed help getting anything out of the Explorer. She sighed. A lot has soured between them since she returned from the Oklahoma Pre-Paid Legal Convention, made the decision to leave Blue Cross, and did so about three months ago. She had taken a leap of faith: committed all of her resources to building her new career as a Pre-Paid Legal Services Independent Associate. At first Carlton was enthusiastic about her commitment to Pre-Paid Legal, but he didn't anticipate the long haul.

Shaun Stephenson sighed. She knew that it was not destined to be a cakewalk. She accepted that being Pre-Paid Legal Associate was business, and had read a lot of books on the pitfalls of startups. It was the reason why she had been banking on funds— owed her from her last job—to keep the lights on and to keep her well afloat until her Pre-paid efforts began paying off.

Today, however, she learnt that the amounts she had been confident in receiving from her old job were in dispute. This meant, that it would be some months before anything got resolved. And while she waited for an outcome, the bills would continue to arrive like time, like tide, that waits on no man. Inadvertently she played a gentle tattoo on the steering column of her Explorer. The was the mortgage... there was the car payment... the insurance... the utilities...

She was the type of a Pre-Paid Legal associate that did not believe in hard selling with a cold eye on the dollar. In her presentations she told her audiences about what Pre-Paid Legal can do to make their lives easier by giving ordinary people equal and affordable access to justice. She always strove to make people she spoke to come to their own decisions about whether or not what she told them about had any value for them. If someone felt her information had value and wanted to buy into the Pre-Paid Legal coverage Shaun sold, then it was up to that person to get back in touch with her. She was never concerned that whom she might educate about Pre-Paid legal might give patronage to another Pre-Paid Legal associate. Shaun didn't mind. She felt that all Pre-Paid legal people were family.

Her experiences from Guyana to Mantua, New Jersey had turned her into a 'people person,' the kind many gravitated to. She endeared herself to others ever so easily.

Shaun turned off the spiritual tape she had been listening to, and whispered, "I am... I am... I am... I know I am. There is no such thing as failure..."

Her phone rang. "Shaun..." she said gently.

"Where are you? On the road?" It was her husband.

"No, I'm in the yard... —I just pulled in..."

"Have anything to bring in?"

"Not really, you know... —I'll be in soon."

"Okay..."

"Were you sleeping?"

"I guess I fell off," he said.

"Catch your rest, you have to get up early. I'll be in just now, okay?"

She was looking beyond the front passenger seat, to the covered swimming pool. For a moment it was open in her mind and she could have heard the voices of her aunts and visiting friends as they frolicked under a summer sun. She closed her eyes and could have seen her dad on his back on a plastic float. She sighed.

What am I going to do? She thought. She sighed despondently. She didn't come all this way to founder against the rocks. No! *This is my test! I did not come this far to file bankruptcy again!*

"No, Shaun!" she hissed to herself. "Don't even think it! —This is going to work! —Pre-paid is going to work! There is no turning back!"

It was not that she wasn't making headway as a Pre-Paid Legal Associate. Of course there were challenges, but there were quite a few things she felt good about. Since returning from Oklahoma she reached out to her team, and helped several new associates achieve the level of manager.

As an Identity Theft Risk Management Specialist with Pre-Paid Legal Incorporated, Shaun also worked with her team to plan and pull off quite a few in-home, and Chamber presentations. There was even one shredding event at a Church where participants were afforded the opportunity to destroy personal documents, lest they fell into the clutches of Identity thieves.

Along with setting the groundwork and building her Pre-Paid legal business, she had also made impressive inroads as an involved entrepreneur. She helped to launch the South Jersey Chapter of the Caribbean American Business Association. It was in this, that she discovered her apparently natural ability to pull people together for a common good.

Her phone was ringing again. She glanced at it. Carlton. "Hi... I'm coming in now."

"Where are you? —Downstairs in your office?"

"No... I'm still outside..."

"Still outside? —You okay, Babes?"

"I'm okay," she said, and just like that she found herself thinking about two thousand and seven —it struck her like an epiphany. "It has turned out to be a year of significant sevens for me..." She whispered. "It is now two thousand and seven and I am thirty-seven... I've been here in America for fourteen years —that is two times seven... I went back home and got married, and now it was our seven-year wedding anniversary." She sighed, "And I've had seven miscarriages... My life has a lot of sevens..."

She shook her head.

Why did this come to me all of a sudden? —What does it mean?

She shrugged. She did not believe in numerology, but it was interesting. *What does it mean?*

Her phone rang again. It was her husband. "I'm coming in now," she told him, and got out of her Explorer.

CHAPTER 28: 2007
The Mantua Story Continues

REFLECTIONS OF GRATITUDE

Sometimes you take a journey... sometimes a journey takes you.
—Harold A. Bascom

When Shaun got inside, she laid her stuff down on the dining table and quickly checked the mail. The carpeted stairway to the bedroom creaked and she knew Carlton was on his way down.

There was another notice from the Mortgage Company and it was opened. "Well..." she muttered below her breath as she felt Carlton's intense warmth as he hugged her and began kissing into her neck.

"Miss you," he murmured in her ear.

She giggled. "Miss you too..."

"Can't wait for Thursday..."

Thursday was the day she would set aside to have quality time with her husband... companionship time. It was a promise she had made, but it was getting difficult to keep. There were so many appointments to make —so many more presentations. It was clear that the money she had hoped to get from last job was not soon forthcoming and the bills were piling up. Collection agencies were beginning to call. Granted it was a trickle, but she aimed to make it stop; she aimed to be on top of it and only through working harder —only through closing memberships would she be able to escape indebtedness.

She turned in his embrace and showed him the letter from the Mortgage Company. "I guess you saw this..."

He sighed, let her go and sat at the table. "Yes... I read it... so... what are you going to do?"

"I'll work something out, Carlton..."

"You hungry? I tried to put together something vegetarian for you..."

She smiled. "No... but thanks. It's after ten..." She shook her head. "Too late for heavy stuff..."

"Coming up to bed now?"

"Soon —but I have to check my emails first..." She bent over and kissed his lips. "Okay?"

"Okay... but don't take too long."

She kissed his lips again. "It will keep..."

. . .

Her office was part of the finished basement of her home. She entered its warmth, walked past the gigantic sectional her mom who lived with them had bought, and entered her office space. She sat before her desktop computer.

She turned it on, but instead of logging onto her email account she just sat there thinking. She thought of her present journey as a Pre-Paid legal professional, and for some reason she found herself thinking about her first Pre-paid Legal mentor... Suzanne Salaam. She would always remember Suzanne... how they had met... how much she had begun to learn about the Pre-paid Legal business with Suzanne... She started thinking too of East Orange and the Hendersons... thinking of her accident... Bindhu... the wedding...

. . .

Suzanne Salaam became a dear friend and confidant, we began attending Pre-Paid Legal training together, began doing private business receptions for associates, business luncheons, going to training on weekends out-of-state as far as Maryland and New York. As such, our teams grew steadily, we became the motivation for our up-line Director, and they wanted to know what we were doing.

We began to do expos and trade shows, I remember getting a booth at the National Black Caucus Convention in Washington DC. It was held at the Convention Center. It was the largest ever show I attended to date. We obtained a lot of leads from that event. Suzanne attained the level of Director and I became Manager. My Trinidadian friend Bindhu had joined my team, and ten other friends had done so too. Susanne and me... —we were both building our businesses on a part-time basis while working our regular jobs.

But my upcoming wedding to Carlton, however, began to slow me down. There were so many things that had to be pulled together for a wedding. I was in New Jersey; he was back in Guyana, and in between there was a mountain of things that had to be done. It was a real challenge choosing a wedding dress... getting my weight down... filling new barrels with foodstuff, icing for the cake, clothing for the wedding party —festive stuff...

At this point I was living in East Orange, the Hendersons had become very dear friends to me and soon I began to feel they were my adopted parents. I worked with Margie at Blue Cross; we were on the Same Team; John, her husband, was ever helpful, and I loved them for their understanding. There I lived alone while working long hours at Blue Cross —saving as much as I could in preparation for my wedding.

And then fate reared its ugly head. Heading home, one afternoon from a visit to my doctor, I drove into an intersection, and a driver ran a red light. I knew that he was going to hit me and hit me hard. I twisted my steering wheel and my world literally exploded.

I was unable to breathe and my shoulders and upper arms ached. My life flashed before me. My eyes burned, and I experienced this strange smell that turned out to be that of the blown airbag of my car, just inches from a steel post. I heard the distant sound of an approaching ambulance... Soon I felt the helping hands helping me onto a stretcher... Shocked and immensely shaken, I thanked God for my good fortune. I was alive... I was blessed.

I was checked over at East Orange General Hospital, given some painkillers, and discharged.

In the meantime, my fully insured car was towed to a workshop. Later the Insurance Company's adjuster looked at it, and submitted his report. To my dismay the insurance company deemed the car 'totaled,' and wrote me a check for an amount that did not cover the total cost of the car I was still making payments on. Now I had no car and a balance of five thousand dollars yet to be paid off on it. So I was left with no other alternative but to enter into a special arrangement with the financing company to repay them over a period of time. And all of this was happening when I was trying to save as much as I could for my wedding to Carlton.

And how was I to get to work now? Even if someone had said to me, "You can use my car," I would have baulked since the experience left me terrified of driving again. But then my good friend Bindhu and her husband, whom I used to car-pool with when I had my car, stepped in and helped... They began taking me to work every morning since we all worked at Blue Cross together.

Bindhu...

She knew that my wedding plans were going to be affected by the loss of my car, and so she began taking to places where I had to shop for my nuptials. She even helped me pack the barrels and put together other needed things — the wedding dress, the bouquet, invitations and other necessities.

Margie Henderson too was involved with the wedding dress. She, Bindhu, and I went dress shopping one weekend at *David's Bridal* only to find I could not fit anything I liked. The size I finally tried on was an 18. Lord! I looked like a stuffed cow in that mirror and vowed to myself that I would *not* look like that, walking down any isle with trim Doods by my side. I told myself that I had to lose weight, and started on a rigorous weight-loss program. Within only three months I dropped thirty pounds, and was able to fit into a size 12 wedding dress.

· · ·

Her phone rang. It was Carlton. "Why are you taking so long to check a few emails, Babes?"

"I'm coming now..." she said and turned off the computer. The emails would have to wait until the next morning.

CHAPTER 29: 2000

A Wedding in Georgetown, Guyana

BASCOM: Let's talk about the wedding.

SHAUN: As I told you before, my wedding day was scheduled for Oct 21, 2000 and my teammates at Blue Cross were excited for me. My friends at work had done a surprise shower. (*Chuckles.*) They gave me a money tree for as a gift for my wedding...

BASCOM: A money tree?

SHAUN: Yes —it was like a real tree, the only difference was the leaves were made out of money —bills. I was so moved with what they did for me I decided to have a barbeque in my East Orange backyard... Sam helped and Margie helped with the cooking, Everyone had a great time, they were happy to that I was finally going to be married to the man I had told them so much about.

BASCOM: I guess this was a time of grand preparations: One month before your big day...

SHAUN: (*Smiling.*) Yes... Since August I had begun shipping barrels home in order that things arrived in Guyana well before the wedding. In the mean time Carlton was handling the location and other details, you know... —The planning was a challenge for us...

BASCOM: Because you were over here and he was back in Guyana...

SHAUN: Yes. For example, initially we were going to print three hundred invitations but quickly realized that there might well be over six hundred people at the wedding if two persons were invited from each family we knew. My family alone—counting in relatives—was large; we could not afford that, so we scaled down the invitations to one hundred and fifty, and averaged that around three hundred would be at the wedding reception. The invitations were to be shared equally among my family and Carlton's; mom got her seventy-five invitations but then she went back to Carlton's mother Joyce for more and almost caused some confusion. (*Shakes her head.*) That mother of mine is something else...

BASCOM: So how did you and Carlton resolve this?

SHAUN: (*Chuckling.*) We resolved it good. We had a big wedding eve bash and invited all who did not get invitations. It turned out to be something like a huge block party...

BASCOM: Wow...

SHAUN: My dad put up tents, organized chairs —tables, and there was a lot to eat and drink.

BASCOM: Tell me about guests. Friends from over here attended?

SHAUN: Margie and John Henderson attended. They arrived on the same flight as Bindhu and Sam who were responsible for my wedding dress, the favors and the bouquets...

BASCOM: Who else flew in from here? —America?

SHAUN: My friend Lynn, who was a witness when I got married to Nigel, flew in on the actual day of the wedding ceremony. My Uncle David and his wife Sharon were also there...

BASCOM: That's the Rahway uncle, right?

SHAUN: Right. Sam's niece Sharmilla and her husband Bill from Trinidad also flew in...

BASCOM: Those were the people you and Carlton stayed with when he had to have his operation in Trinidad, right... —So, when did you travel to Guyana for your wedding?

SHAUN: I traveled home one week before the big day to make sure all arrangements were in order. It was going to be a poolside wedding, with a live band... It was going to be a catered event... —we even had a decorator who ended up saving my wedding cake...

BASCOM: (*Baffled.*) Why your wedding cake had to be saved?

SHAUN: (*Chuckles.*) That was something else, I tell you... Okay... After the cake was baked, the plan was to ice it in Guyana...

BASCOM: Hold on, hold on... I need to get something straight here. You say the plan was to ice it in Guyana; so the cake wasn't baked in Guyana.

SHAUN: No. The cake was baked right here in America. Sam, Bindhu's husband, baked it, and I brought it home with me on the plane...

BASCOM: So the plan was to ice them *in* Guyana —continue...

SHAUN: The girl who we made arrangements with to do the cake did a lot of nonsense! First she put the cake in the refrigerator instead of leaving it outside. Then she used up all of the good icing I had brought over other cakes —leaving the wedding cake for last...

BASCOM: In other words there was the wedding cake and then there were lesser cakes, and the wedding cake should have been given priority...

SHAUN: Exactly! This girl used up all the good icing on other cakes, waited until the night before the wedding to ice my wedding cake, and had to buy local icing that was no good, to do the wedding cake. (*Shakes her head.*) What happened next was like a tragedy in itself...

BASCOM: What happened?

SHAUN: The local icing she started using on the wedding cake did not work well and the actual cake began falling apart...

BASCOM: The night before the wedding. Wow!

SHAUN: I almost bust into tears when she called me over and showed me what was happening...

BASCOM: So that's when your decorator saved the day...

SHAUN: I showed her what was happening to the cake and she said, "Don't worry, Shaun... I'll fix it..."

BASCOM: And she did.

SHAUN: Yes. She dressed the cake up and no one knew the trouble.

. . .

Bindhu and Sam really worked at my wedding —cooking all the food and helping my Mom. Sam, who was a chef, made sure everything in the kitchen was in great shape.

On the day before the nuptials, my dad had a large tent erected in front of our house in Crane Village. This was to facilitate a big celebration for many of our friends and neighbors who wouldn't be in the City for the actual wedding. Bindhu and Sam made over two hundred puris for that evenings feast, and by the time they were finished, her feet were swollen from standing all day

And then it was Saturday. My wedding day had arrived and there was yet much to do if you know how wedding days are. I had an appointment to get my hair done at a salon my cousin Sandra owned in Georgetown City. It had all been planned before I flew in. But you know what they say about the best-laid plans of mouse and men?

My friend Lynn and I hired a taxi to take us and bring us back, so early that morning we were driven to the salon only to discover that Sandra was not there yet. It was about 7: A.M. The wedding was at 4: P.M. My hair had to be done in time for me to get back over the river to be dressed, and after that cross back to the City and then all the way to the East Coast and the Ocean View Hotel where everything was scheduled to take place. We feared time would be tight.

Sandra finally arrived and we proceeded to the sink to wash my hair, and that was when the lights went out: Power outage. I could *not* believe it! And there was no telling when it would be back.

. . .

BASCOM: And what she did?

SHAUN: She began to make anxious phone calls to borrow a generator and time was going... (*Shakes her head.*) At this time, it's about 1: P.M. and no generator. At 2: P.M. she finally got through to someone with one, and it became crunch time. It ended up with three people working on my head...

BASCOM: Working frantically...

SHAUN: I wouldn't say that — not frantically, but very quickly and expertly. I have to give them that. It was about 2:45 P.M. when I got done, and the taxi was waiting to take me home all flustered, back through the City and over the pontoon bridge back to my parents' home in Crane Scheme...

BASCOM: Were you worried that the bridge might have been open for river traffic and that would have messed your time some more?

SHAUN: No. The taxi driver assured us that the bridge would be no problem — that everything was going to be okay, and got us back in record time. When we were approaching my home I saw my dad and his Uncle Selwyn walking towards us. I asked the taxi to stop and my father saw us. "Why aren't you ready, Dad?" I asked him. He said he had to go get a hair cut. In my mind I swore. In my mind it was like, *Jeeze! —It's almost 3: 15 P.M. —there's no time to play and he's making it seem like 'no big deal!* I got home and began to get ready, Margie did my make-up and made sure my accessories were in place.

BASCOM: What time is it now?

SHAUN: It was now about 4: 45 P.M. but I was ready. Tasha, my stepsister, was maid of honor; she along with my Mom came in the car with me. We got to Ocean View about 4:30 P.M.

BASCOM: You were late...

SHAUN: But Carlton was already there, but Dad was nowhere in sight. This upset me further and I was about to go ahead and get married without him there. I told myself that I would have my brother Glen or my uncle David take me down the isle. Then Glenn received a frantic phone call from my father saying that he was on his way and that I should please wait.

BASCOM: I guess that by then you were really strung out...

SHAUN: That is really putting it mildly. (*Chuckles; shakes her head.*) Everyone tried to calm me down. In my mind I'm saying, *He has done it again! —On my wedding day!*

BASCOM: But he came...

SHAUN: But I was so mad I didn't want to speak to him!

BASCOM: (*Laughing.*) And so he tried to calm you down...

SHAUN: (*Laughing too.*) He apologized and all that, and in the end I took a deep breath and forgave him...

. . .

I walked down the configured aisle between the hotel and the poolside where the ceremony isle.

I was composed and Carton seemed so too, and the ceremony went very well. The kids blew bubbles, lots of pictures were taken at the Ocean View hotel, but I needed to have a few more taken in the Botanical Gardens and at our Cuffy National Monument since we had some daylight left. After those pictures we headed back to the hotel for the live-band wedding reception that was attended by over three hundred people.

My Uncle Gervy was the Master of Ceremonies and he did an extraordinary job. I was so happy to see my former boss, Anita Sinclair, along with some other old friends and acquaintances from the bank. These were people I hadn't seen for over seven years.

I think of Indra Rupan who did a solo for me and Carlton at the reception. She was a childhood friend whom I knew since I was about twelve —thirteen. At that time she and I sang together in the church that used to be held under her parents' home in Crane Village. She even gave a little speech...

. . .

BASCOM: You remember what she said?

SHAUN: "I've know Carlton and Shaundal for eighteen years..." That was how I think she began, and when she said that I felt like I was fifty years old. Everyone, except for the generation I went back and met, knew us as kids growing up. But everyone had a great time. I went around and personally thanked everyone. This entire event was recorded for posterity. I think everything went well despite the earlier hiccups... and the girls who attended really looked beautiful —and that is something I felt good about and I'll tell you why. I had Sam buy a lot of raw cloth in Trinidad for me, and he had it shipped over to Guyana so that all the girls who were to attend would have had the same material, you know... and Carlton's sister sewed all the dresses.

BASCOM: You actually outfitted your bridesmaids —that's good.

SHAUN: Not only the girls, but I bought my mother's dress... my mother-in-law' dress... my sister-in-law's dress... and Carlton actually helped with the men. We did it because we knew how hard things are in Guyana. People can't afford much with the economy being the way it was —still is... Deep within me, I saw my wedding as an opportunity to give back, more than anything else...

BASCOM: That's good...

SHAUN: It was indeed a memorable day in my life... and the best part was, we paid cash for everything and had no debt after the fun.

The day after the wedding and everything, we had a family day at *Splashmins*, a get-away picnicking and swimming resort off the Linden-Soesdyke Highway. All my friends who traveled in for the wedding had a day to relax and continue having fun at the creek.

BASCOM: What about the honeymoon?

SHAUN: I had to travel back to New Jersey that following Monday so there was no honeymoon really. We had to put that off until later... (*Shaun suddenly starts to laugh —really laugh.*)

BASCOM: Want to share that?

SHAUN: I'm going to share it with you though I'm not sure it will be appropriate for the book...

BASCOM: Tell me —then we'll decide.

SHAUN: After everything was over and Carlton and I retired to a special suite at the hotel—compliments of the management for us using the facility... I started changing out of my wedding dress... and when I got down to my underwear I realized that throughout the ceremony —the reception everything, my underwear was on totally wrong —I was wearing... (*Laughs as she speaks.*) One of the legs of my panties on my waist...

BASCOM: (*Laughing.*) That is one detail that summarizes the tension a woman can experience on her wedding day... (*Laughing.*) Do we put it in? —If we can do so tastefully —(*Shrugs.*) Why not?

SHAUN: And on the following Monday I traveled back to East Orange and went to work the next day. Of course I brought back favors for the Blue Cross team I was in. Everyone got something. But they all wanted to know why I came back so soon.

CHAPTER 30: 2001
Destination Owings Mills, Maryland

Owings Mills is also home to around a dozen major shopping centers and numerous office buildings. In the center of Owings Mills is Owings Mills Town Center, an enclosed shopping mall. The Owings Mills Town Center, which opened in 1986, features more than 200 stores, including its anchors of JC Penny, Boscovs, and Macy's. The Owings Mills Town Center is located less than one mile from a the Baltimore Metro Subway station.

Back from her wedding, Shaun felt very determined to succeed as an Independent Pre-Paid legal associate and reconnected with Suzanne Salaam who had never taken a break from the entrepreneurial venture. They began working once again as a Pre-Paid legal duo.

Shaun hosted a private Business Reception at her East Orange apartment, twelve people showed up, and she was able to sell six memberships. This excited her. In her mind it was a sure sign that things were picking up —that she would be successful in her Pre-Paid Legal endeavors. Her confidence was kicked into a higher gear, and soon she began to question the relevance of her nine-to-five job. She told herself that she could do better —that she could do without it. She told herself that the time she spent at a desk at her regular job was time she could have been using to grow her Pre-Paid Legal business that was turning out to be a sure thing! *I need a break from Blue Cross!* she thought. *This is the break I've been waiting for! I will make my Pre-Paid Legal business worth the while! I'll be independent! —My own Boss!*

Soon she and Suzanne began getting support from a PPLSI leader who lived in Virginia. Through conversations with this individual, they envisioned great opportunities to expand —to grow in Maryland. From the sound of it, the compensation for operating as Pre-paid Legal Independent Associates out of that state, promised to be great.

. . .

Suzanne and me attended a Pre-Paid Legal Leadership Conference in Baltimore, Maryland, and were both fired up and ready to move there and build our business. We really liked Maryland as a state. When we compared it to New Jersey, we thought, *Advantage Maryland!* That the rent was so low in the Old Line State, helped to tip the scale. So we made the big decision: we were going to take our Pre-Paid Legal chances in Owings Mills, Maryland, and I took a leap of Faith and gave Blue Cross two weeks notice. I left them that August.

Mom arrived in the United States that same month, and on the day that Suzanne and I would be traveling to be part of an Event in Washington DC. So after I picked my mom up from the airport and dropped her off at my aunt in Plainfield, Suzanne and I drove to the Evergreen State, and attended the National Black Caucus event.

. . .

On September 11th, while packing in preparation to move to Owings Mills, there was a newsflash on the TV in my bedroom. I saw a jet plane crashing into one of the twin towers, and soon after the tall buildings collapsed before my very eyes. I remember how surreal it was seeing an unfolding tragedy. What was most interesting, is that I had made plans to take my mom to New York that very weekend to visit other sites in Manhattan and see the Twin Towers.

At Blue Cross, the office I worked in was so positioned I could have seen the famous skyscrapers over In Manhattan. All I had to do was look out the window behind my desk. There were times when I was at work so early I was able to see the sun coming up beyond the twin towers.

I tried to put September 11th behind me since I had to focus on my new venture.

In my preparing to leave, the Margie and John Henderson were sad to see me go but wished me well. They told me, however, that should I need a place to stay whenever I was in New

Jersey, their home would always be open to me. "Or if you decide that you want to come back to New Jersey and need a place to rent," John said. "Give us a call first, okay?"

"Okay," I said, but in my mind there would be no turning back. In my mind Owings Mills was it! It was where my business would take off. I was determined to follow through with my plans, and a few months later me and my mom got into the Ford Explorer I had leased with Bindhu's co-signed help, met with Suzanne and her two daughter in her Caravan, and started the long drive to Owings Mills, Maryland.

. . .

In Owings Mils, Maryland, I rented a town house and Susanne rented one too. They were both in a beautiful gated community that was fairly new and set among trees.

Mine, and Susanne's too, had all the amenities anyone would need in a home. I did not have to go to the Laundromat. It had two bedrooms two baths that were both very spacious. That town-house was simply splendid. My mother, new to North American luxuries, was excited.

While there, Susanne arranged for her daughter's transfer to schools in Maryland and my mom had started looking to find a job in Owings Mills. Between looking she took care of Susanne's daughters.

We settled in at Owings Mills. I joined a few women's groups and began making phone call —sending letters introducing the Pre-Paid legal entity to organizations, and there were favorable responses that seemed to show interest. Susanne was doing the same too.

Then the bottom of our enterprise started to sag. To our dismay the Pre-Paid Legal person in Virginia whom had assured that he would be on hand to help us make beneficial contacts, build a team, and get the appropriate training as Independent Associates, reneged on his promises. It didn't take Suzanne and I long to realize we were on our own with no lifelines. But I was not going to wait until the entire bottom of our hasty enterprise fell out from under us before I did something to help myself from falling. What was troubling was the fact that I was renting a townhouse in Owings Mills and whatever money I had would soon run out.

I had a large amount of determination, however, and Suzanne and I continued to push our Pre-paid Legal endeavors. But the weeks went by and we closed nothing! It seemed that no one was interested in what we were sharing. The excuses came fast: "Not right now... "We'll get back to you... "Let's touch bases in a few months..."

I began to feel a fool —gullible.

Nothing was coming in, and my cash reserves were almost gone and. It did not have even a couple of months to last... So I began looking for a Job, and caught a break: I got a call from a third party insurance processing company. They offered me a job based on my Blue Cross experience. For them, I brought a lot of experience to their table.

· · ·

SHAUN: It came, however, with a twenty-thousand-dollar-annual pay-cut since in the South you made less and living was cheaper. This only compounded things for me since what I was being paid was not covering my bills. I was in desperate financial straights.

So One night I called home to Carlton... and told him that things were bad for me —that I hadn't any money... He insisted that I came back home —that he was going to send a ticket for me —that he was going to help me since his business in Georgetown City was really booming... (*Sighs.*) So I asked for two weeks of no-pay leave and I flew home to Guyana that Easter, dead broke, disappointed, and some-what depressed... Carlton welcomed me with open arms. I spent two weeks and he did some projects... (*Shakes her head.*) Believe it or not... Carlton raised seven thousand U.S. dollars for me to take care of my outstanding bills...

BASCOM: Fantastic... and then you returned to Maryland...

SHAUN: Yes... to discover that I was pregnant, and that it wasn't coming along well...

BASCOM: You're going to tell me about that?

SHAUN: I might as well... (*Takes a deep breath.*) About eight weeks after I returned to Owings Mills and started back on the job with the third party insurance company, I started feeling sick. While working one day I began to feel nauseated. Along with that there was a lot of pain in my pelvis area —and this continued a few days... And then spotting began with more intense pain. One day I was at work but pain below my belly was so bad. The bleeding and pain got worse so I had to leave. When I got home and told my mom about it, she became concerned and suggested I went to the hospital.

BASCOM: But could you drive at this stage?

SHAUN: Well my mom couldn't... —so I had to drive myself to the hospital... It took all I had to make it. Since I was new to the Maryland area it took me some time finding the hospital...

BASCOM: But you made it...

SHAUN: Yes —and saw a doctor, who did an ultra-sound, did and blood and urine test, and confirmed that I had been pregnant...

BASCOM: *Had* been.

SHAUN: (*Nods.*) Lost the baby... He gave me medication for the pain and I returned to work the next day...

BASCOM: The *next* day...

SHAUN: Yep. I wasn't feeling well but I had to go in to work... —I was new on that job remember? I couldn't get the time off...

BASCOM: Tough.

SHAUN: I didn't linger there too long however... Soon afterwards my friend Bindhu helped my mother to find a job as a live-in nanny back in New Jersey, so Mom left... Soon after that, however, Carlton's mom and his sister arrived in America and were staying with me in Owings Mill...

BASCOM: I guess it was very difficult accommodating them...

SHAUN: Because of my busy life with work and trying to make ends meet in Maryland... (*Shakes her hear.*) It definitely was not a good time for my mother and sister-in-law's vacation. For Aunt Joyce t was especially hard since her daughter had left her with me and had gone to New York in the hope of finding work there. So Aunt Joyce was left home alone by herself in that lonely Maryland townhouse most of the time.

BASCOM: You call your mother-in-law, Aunt Joyce...

SHAUN: Yes... I felt bad about not being able to entertain her, you know —take her sight seeing and shopping and the like... It started to feel pointless —stupid! ...So I said to myself, "Shaun, why don't you simply break this lease, pack your bags, and go back to New Jersey?"

BASCOM: And that's what you did...

SHAUN: But first I called Mr. Frank Fee of Blue Cross...

BASCOM: Who was he in the Blue Cross structure?

SHAUN: He was the V.P. of Customer Service —I had kept in touch with him and other key people.

BASCOM: That was wise.

SHAUN: Mr. Fee knew me well. He told me that the Blue Cross office was at the new location in Mount laurel and it was coming well. He said that he was glad I called him since they really needed experience people like myself...

BASCOM: There you go...

SHAUN: I also reached out to Jackie Jennifer; she was a V.P. whom I got to know very well... (*Makes an open-palmed gesture.*) So...

BASCOM: They called you back...

SHAUN: I was offered my job back and the timing was perfect.

BASCOM: Why?

SHAUN: Because my good friend Bindhu was also stationed in Mt Laurel at that time... —she was doing employee training... —So I told Suzanne I was going to take my job back at Blue Cross... (*Shrugs.*) But things just wasn't working out with our Pre-Paid Legal venture —"I'm not abandoning Pre-Paid Legal, Suzanne," I told her. "But... I got to do this..."

BASCOM: Did she understand?

SHAUN: Yes, she did. She later returned to New Jersey as well.... (*Shrugs.*) So I broke my Lease in Owings Mills. It was only eight months into it...

BASCOM: It was a one-year lease...

SHAUN: And so I lost my security deposit which was what I really needed... Anyway, I moved back to New Jersey.

BASCOM: Big move...

SHAUN: I think I'm jumping the gun here, so let me back up. I left Owings Mills with my in-laws for New Jersey, but it wasn't the big move as yet.

BASCOM: You hadn't actually given up the place as yet.

SHAUN: No, because even though I moved back to New Jersey tentatively, I hadn't found an apartment back in New Jersey yet, and stayed a short time with Bindhu in Mount Laurel until I found a place to rent in Maple Shade...

CHAPTER 31: 2002
Maple Shade, New Jersey

THE TRAIL TO BANKRUPTCY

What is now Maple Shade was originally formed as Chester Township on November 6, 1668, and was also known as Cropwell Township from June 5, 1690 through February 22, 1699. Chester was incorporated as one of New Jersey's initial 104 townships by an Act of the New Jersey Legislature on February 21, 1798. Portions of the township were taken to form Cinnaminson Township (March 15, 1860) and Moorestown Township (March 11, 1922). The name was changed to Maple Shade township as of November 6, 1945, based on the results of a referendum passed that same day.

In July 2002, Bindhu, Sam and their family helped me move my stuff out of from Owings Mills to the townhouse I was able to rent in Maple Shade, and I soon settled into my second stint at Blue Cross.

Despite the challenges I had faced with my Pre-Paid Legal business, it was, however was still on my mind. "Maybe..." I told myself, "I'll be to sell some memberships here in Maple Shade." I guess at heart I was a Pre-Paid Legal person. I told myself, however, that it had to stay on the backburner until I was able to get my finances in order.

I knew I had stepped into debt, and debt was quicksand. I was hoping that being reemployed by Blue Cross was the hand to grab onto, and as such, focused on getting back my rhythm with the giant company. I grasped the new benefit structure and system very quickly, and soon after, my supervisor began giving me special projects and added responsibilities. I was also permitted to work Overtime and I was happy about this because there were a lot of bills that had to be brought current. There were even bills that dated back to when I lived in Montclair. I was desperately trying to keep myself afloat, but even with the overtime work I did, I was finding it hard to keep on top of rising financial obligations...

. . .

BASCOM: The balance never seemed to get less...

SHAUN: (*Echoes.*) Never seemed to get less... — minimum payments were all I could have afforded to make on many of them. I had even tried credit counseling, but... (*Makes an open-palmed gesture of hopelessness.*)...My credit score was going down hill fast. (*Takes a deep breath and continues.*) One Sunday afternoon I had just dropped my mother off at the Hamilton, New Jersey Train Station. She was going back to her live-in job in Bernardsville, New Jersey. As I lingered with her, I saw a yellow smiley-face flyer that read, *FAIR CREDIT ALLIANCE! —For Free Consultation & Debt Consolidation —Call Monica McGill!* God! —I was so excited to have found the information that I called—even though it was Sunday—and left a message...

BASCOM: She called you back...

SHAUN: The very next day, and we scheduled an appointment.

. . .

NOVEMBER. Shaun Stephenson pulled up to the Hamilton office where she had a scheduled consultancy appointment with Monica McGill. She entered the building, followed the simple direction and quickly found Fair Credit Alliance, and Monica McGill stood before her desk with a bright smile that rivaled her eyes.

"Welcome, Shaun," she said brightly.

"Hi, Monica..."

"Sit down, please..." McGill said and sat behind her huge desk that was slightly cluttered.

"Thank you..."

"Cold outside eh?" Monica said easily, a ray of spilled sunlight on her light skin, and another highlighting her hair pulled back in a bun. "Now, Shaun... this session we're having now is merely the consultancy...

"At this stage I am just going to listen to you and afterwards tell you what I think about your situation —suggest a remedial path. After that, it will be up to your call as to whether you'll continue with me as the person who will help you..."

"I understand..."

"So... we'll begin by you telling me about your financial situation... —just talk, girl... tell me in any way want to..."

"Okay..." Shaun said and began to speak. She felt at ease as she spoke to Monica McGill. She felt as if Monica was an old friend. She told it all.

At last, Monica McGill said, "Listen, Shaun... *your* goal is to get out of debt, okay?"

"Yes, before my husband arrives," Shaun said in a low voice.

"What's that?"

"I was saying that my goal is to get out of debt before my husband arrives in America." She shook her head. "I don't want us to be still saddled with bills from a previous marriage. I don't think it will be fair to him..."

"I agree." Monica cleared her throat lightly. "Shaun... Unless you can somehow increase your income... you'll need to file for bankruptcy."

"I can try to find more overtime work to get on top of the bills..."

"And what?" Monica said flatly. "Kill yourself with overwork before your husband comes?"

Shaun Stephenson sighed.

"The longer you struggle to pay off these bills..." Monica McGill shrugged. "The worse it will get..."

"I still want to give it a try —working longer overtime hours to see if I can pay these bills off..."

"Okay... But if it doesn't work out, you know where I am. I'm here to help you..."

"Thanks..."

Shaun left —determined to do what she had to do bring her bills down to a manageable level. Bankruptcy was going to be her last resort.

. . .

Working overtime did not help much and three months later, February 2003, Shaun sat once again before Monica McGill.

"You have the pay stubs and all the things I asked you to get..."

"Yes..." Shaun reached into her workbag and brought out a large, manila envelope. "I have all that here —pay stubs... all the bills I owe...

Monica opened the envelope and leafed through the documents. "Good..." She said, reached into a drawer of her desk and brought out a new file folder. "I ran your credit..."

"I guess it didn't look good..."

"Nope. It doesn't, Shaun... your credit score is below four hundred..."

"That's bad... I know..."

Monica drew a desktop calculator, gathered the bills and the pay stubs that Shaun brought. Her slender fingers flipped over the keypad of the calculator... "What I'm beginning to see here, Shaun... is that you are barely making it keep afloat when I look at your current expenses..." Monica Gill stopped and looked directly at Shaun.

"I guess you knew I would be back..." Shaun said.

Monica laughed knowingly. "What can I say, Shaun?"

"I guess I should go ahead and file for bankruptcy..."

"I do..."

"Okay, how do I do that?"

"How do we do that? —You're going to file the case Pro Se —that means you won't require an attorney —you're going to represent yourself, okay?"

"Pro Se, okay..."

And that's what she did: filed bankruptcy, and began piecing her life back together again.

CHAPTER 32: 2002 · 2003
The Maple Shade Story Continues

SELFLESS EXECUTIVE SUPPORT, AND DOOD'S ARRIVAL

I got a call from Suzanne who by this time had moved back to New Jersey. She sounded excited.

"Shaun!" she said with school girlish excitement. "Listen to this! —Listen to this!"

"Calm down, Suzanne! I'm listening," I said.

"I met a Pre-Paid Legal Executive Director named David Allen in Cancun, and he said that he wouldn't mind helping me in my Pre-Paid Legal business— I'm so sorry you couldn't make Cancun, girl..."

"Well you know... I missed it by a mile —but you're telling me about this David Allen person —what? He said he would help you? You're sure? Don't forget what happened in Maryland, Suzanne!"

"Shaun! —This guy is genuine —trust me on this!"

"Okay..."

"Shaun, I want us to meet him together! If he can help us spark our business again —why not?"

"Meet him where?"

"Philly," she said.

I did not live far from Philadelphia so we arranged to meet whoever this David Allen was that weekend.

It turned that she was right. David Allen came over quite genuinely to me. He was a real soft-spoken helper and almost fatherly. I learned so much from him just that one day. David Allen re-introduced Pre-Paid Legal from a new point of view. Because of his background in business he revealed new approaches towards building a respectable and trustworthy Pre-Paid Legal Services business. His concepts were very enlightening. He stressed two very important things: joining organizations in order to meet people, and—most importantly—follow the System Pre-Paid Legal Services already has in place.

For me, being an Independent Associate with Pre-Paid Legal Services Incorporated was once more a rekindled passion. I began sharing Pre-Paid Legal information with a few people at work. Then I decided to make use of one of David Allen's tips and joined my first organization: the New Jersey State Chamber of all places. I called a few people and was able to get in touch with Mr. Ken Evans by phone. He was the State Chamber's Memberships Representative. He provided me some basic information about the organization, and suggested that we meet so that he might share details of the chamber with me.

. . .

BASCOM: And you met...

SHAUN: We had a great meeting... Ken was a very pleasant and honest individual... He shared a lot with me... about how the Chamber works and its benefits... explained that it was where a lot of networking took place...

BASCOM: Networking...

SHAUN: Then, I knew nothing about networking—but I got along well with people, so I was sure this networking business was going to be easy for me —at least that was what I thought... So, having joined the State Chamber, I was ready for the 'networking experience.' David coached me from California by phone about the pros and cons of networking... I began to attend functions and events that allowed me to meet —network. Things were coming along quite well—business was picking up... I began recruiting more people to the team that Suzanne and I were building. Everyone we recruited seemed dedicated and wanted to build their dreams. Oh, man! Things were looking good. We were having private business receptions at my apartment and other associates homes... — David Allen even flew once to help me for one week of activities that we had put together...

BASCOM: How large was the team?

SHAUN: About fifteen strong and counting... And then something happened that made me think, *Oh no! —Not Owings Mills again! Please! Not again!*

BASCOM: Tell me about that...

SHAUN: I planned this huge event —something like a business seminar, and rented space at the Cherry Hill Hilton...

BASCOM: What capacity space are you talking about?

SHAUN: For five hundred people. So I paid for the space after inviting a few very important people —this man Stanley El, the host of the American Dream Show, whom I had met March of 2003. He supported me and was on the Agenda to speak. Pre-Paid Legal's Platinum Director Russell Peden even drove from Virginia for this event... In terms of promoting this event, we had done up over one thousand flyers and got them out... (*Nods.*) Do you want to guess how many people showed up for that event —not counting invited guest speakers and Platinum Director Russell Peden?

BASCOM: Ten?

SHAUN: Nope...

BASCOM: How many?

SHAUN: (*Touches the tip of her index finger to the tip of her thumb.*) Zero.

BASCOM: Wow.

SHAUN: (*Shaking her head.*) It was simply devastating... But you know that saying, 'when you get lemons, you make lemonade?' (*Chuckles.*) Russell Peden rose to the occasion and made something out of the disappointment: He converted the stillborn 'Business Seminar' into our own in-house training session... He even treated those who were there to lunch —and over lunch he spoke about how important a third party was when introducing the Pre-paid Legal service to people. Later, he continued teaching us about approach, recruiting, exposure and follow-up as it relates to direct marketing, but in specific context of the Pre-Paid Legal Services business. The disappointment turned out to be a blessing in disguise...

· · ·

Though our big event flopped, our team was determined to carry on. We were young in the business and knew we needed a lot of training. So we began attending the Maple Shade business briefings, Fast Start Training, and other local coaching courses that were available. By that time I had also become a member of the Cherry Hill Chamber.

I am proud to say that I was able to help several team members achieve the level of senior associates and Managers. At this time also, I had a special promotion that allowed me to achieve the level of Director.

In order to boost our team, I planned some Pre-Paid Legal Services out-reach events and PPLSI Executive Director David agreed to fly in from California and help. This, however, was around the same time my Dad had arrived very ill in America. It was also around the same time my husband was scheduled to go in to the U.S. Embassy In Georgetown, Guyana for his Permanent Resident visa, and I had to be there with him. I traveled to South America, attended the interview with him, everything went smoothly, and he was ready to return for a life with me after ten years of us being apart.

We had gotten married seven years after I came to America; we had spent another three years apart due to me being denied Citizenship the first time I had applied: I had filed too early and was deemed ineligible. I later refiled for U.S. citizenship, and was finally sworn in on June 25, 2002. It had been a long time coming.

. . .

We arrived in America and Carlton seemed not to be in awe. He acted as though he'd been here before. As we headed, towards immigration, however I guess it began to dawn on him that he was in the great U.S. of A. At last we stood before the Immigration officer and I showed both our documents. The officer welcomed him to America. With his documents from the U.S. Embassy in Georgetown, he was soon in the processing office while I headed to claim our baggage.

In a few minutes he joined me as I we waited by the winding baggage carousel. I said to Carlton, "Do you remember we're going on a Cruise to Mexico?"

"Yes... I remember... I remember you told me about this cruise you had to go on right around our wedding anniversary... —I guess that will be nice...."

"But it is a business, cruise, Doods; remember that too, okay?"

"Meaning?"

"Meaning that on it, we won't be together on the cruise all..."

"Are you trying to tell me something, Babes?"

"No-no..."

"A business cruise... so who would be going on this cruise?"

"Well... members of the Pre-Paid Legal, Legal Eagles team... —Mr. David Allen, Mrs. Fran Alexander, Mr. Russell Peden... —you know, other people in the business..."

"Okay..."

"Doods, you don't sound very excited."

"Well... I just thought we'd be having time together..."

"We *would* be having time together, Doods. —You'll be with me..."

"Okay, Babes..." he said somewhat reluctantly.

We got our bags and headed for clearance. The officer checked our passports... Carlton's documents, everything was in order and we headed out to 'arrivals.'

My faithful friend Bindhu was waiting there to welcome us,

and take us to her home where my Mitsubishi Galant was parked. I had bought it after giving up the Explorer. Making the monthly payments on it was not easy, and I told myself, that when Carlton got here I didn't want to be saddled with too many bills.

₵ℍ₳ℙₜℰℝ 33: 2007
The Mantua Story Continues

MEETING STANLEY AND CHRISTINA

8:30 A.M. Shaun Stephenson, dressed in white, drove the new Ford Explorer into the driveway of her Mantua, New Jersey home. She parked and turned off the ignition. In the silent wake of the Explorer's switched off engine, she listened to a piano composition by her spiritual mentor and good friend Stanley El.

She first met him four years ago. She had been speaking to a few workmates by the water cooler one mid-morning about her part-time Pre-Paid Legal Services business, when another co-worker coming by, paused briefly and then continued on her way. Shaun didn't think of it.

A few days later, however, when Shaun was leaving for home, she fell into step with another Blue Cross employee who was also heading to the parking lot.

"Shaun," the girl said. " I couldn't help it; I overheard you talking about your Pre-Paid Legal business the other day, and I wanted to let you know that I know someone who may be a good contact for you..."

"Is he doing the same thing? Is he with Pre-Paid Legal?"

"I don't think so, but he does a radio show at Rowan University called the American Dream... —he might be helpful..."

"What's his name?"

"Stanley El," she said. "If you're interested I can give you his number. He is the Director for Economic Development for the City of Woodbury..."

Shaun remembered...

She took the contact information gracefully and thanked the co-worker.

Radio? She had never thought of a broadcast medium being incorporated into what she did as a PPLSI Independent Associate. But to be on a radio show meant publicity, and thought that something very opportune may well come out of it.

So she called to speak to Mr. Stanley El, and got him on the phone. He told her a bit about himself and what he did, and she requested a meeting with him. He agreed to meet her at the Woodbury Township office.

To her, Woodbury, New Jersey, was new territory, but she found it by using Map Quest. She drove from Maple Shade, eventually got there, found parking close to the address, and she walked to the Township building. She said hello to the ladies on the first floor, asked where she might find Mr. El's office and was directed to the second floor.

She remembered...

She found the office, rapped on the door, and a heavy voice told her to come on in. She entered and saw this cheerful man with wide eyes in shirt and tie. He laughed good-naturedly —rich and deep from his chest, and rose to greet her. "You must be Shaun Stephenson," he said.

"Yes, I am."

"I am Stanley El..."

"How are you, sir?"

He laughed his rich laugh and said, "Extraordinary."

"I like that," she said chuckling.

He stepped forward and shook her hand. "It's so good to meet you," he said. There was a boyish twinkle in his wide eyes. "Take a seat —make yourself comfortable..."

"Thank you for taking the time to meet with me," she said.

He laughed again. "It's no trouble." he said and sat over from her. "I am glad you made it... —so Shaun, and I must tell you it's quite an unusual name for a girl, how can I help you?"

"Well... If you first tell me more about what you do, I'll then tell you what I do. Like that, you'll be able to say in what ways you might help me..."

He laughed again. "Well put, Shaun —is it okay if I call you Shaun?"

"It's okay..."

She sat in her Ford Explorer and remembered that first day she had met Stanley El...

He explained that he was volunteering for the City —helping

it on the right track for economic development. He told me about his media background and that he was the Host of a radio show. In their talk it came out that he did not go to college and something about this casual admission struck a positive chord within Shaun. She too had not gone to college in America but it was not stopping her on her path to success.

In the course of their initial talk she told him about her coming to America, about some of the things she did, and about her dream: to one day help make a difference in people's lives by creating opportunities through business.

She then told him about her association with Pre-Paid Legal Services Incorporated and that how, through it, she believed her dream was going to be realized.

"I am humbled by your sincerity and your obvious passion, Shaun," he said. "I am touched because your American dream is more than the mere acquisition of holding a good job and owning a home..."

"Thank you..."

"As a young woman with a goal that is almost spiritual," he continued. "I would love to have you on my radio show..."

"I would appreciate that..."

She remembered how excited she had been. It was going to be the very first time she would be on radio.

She remembered.

He even wrote an article about her in his column on Business and personal development in the *Courier Post*.

She remembered...

Carlton had not yet arrived in America, but she told him over the phone that once he came over, there was someone she had met who she thought might be able to help him get grounded as a graphic artist in America. One week after he came over, he got to know Stanley.

Shaun remembered...

After that initial meeting, Shaun lost touch of Stanley for three years until she met him again under rather unusual circumstances. Her father had died and she was taking her mom around to gather some last minute stuff to take back to Guyana, South America, for the funeral. It was raining that day and they were driving along Route 45.

They were coming up on a gentleman who to her, looked familiar. He was walking in the rain as though the day was sunny and bright. Shaun drove past him slowly, and saw it was Stanley El whom she had met before.

She slowed down and shouted his name.

He looked over to the vehicle, and smiled broadly.

She remembered his smile; she never forgot his wide eyes. She pulled over and stopped. He came over and he was soaking wet. "Hello, Mr. El!" she said excitedly. "It's been a long time! —Why are you walking in the rain? —Let me give you a lift!"

He laughed, passed on the lift, and blessed the downpour.

"So where have you been, Mr. El?"

Stanley El laughed and said that he had been in Woodbury all the while.

"Mr. El," Shaun said. "It's so good to see you! What timing! —Oh! This is my Mom!"

He shook her mother's hand.

"You're sure you don't want to come out of the rain?" my mom asked.

Stanley laughed. "I'm sure..."

Shaun told him that her dad had passed, that they were traveling back to Guyana the next day to take care of things, and he offered his sympathies to her and her mom. "You and your mom take care, and everything will be well with God's Grace..." Stanley said.

"I'll be back in a week, Mr. El. I'll call you on my return."

"That will be extraordinary, Shaun..."

They exchanged telephone numbers, said their goodbyes, and Stanley El continued on in the rain.

A few weeks later their acquaintanceship was rekindled. Stanley was willing and ready to support her in whatever endeavors she embarked on. She told him about PPLSI and how things then stood. By that time Stanley had started The Wealth Creation magazine. He gave her a few editions and the stories were inspirational.

They began to talk more about God and man's purpose here on earth. Their conversations were deep. She reconnected with Stanley at a spiritual crossroads of her life —at a point when there was so much turmoil, and this included my Dad's leaving and subsequent passing. There was an emptiness crying for closure. She was searching for answers, for purpose. There had to be more to Life —there had to be a deeper understanding of God.

That Christmas Stanley El gave her a gift, a book: *Unveiled Mysteries*. It opened her eyes to deep spiritual things she had long felt, and she made a commitment to the seeking of Universal Truth. There was something inside her that desired to know more about GOD —something within her that yearned for a closer relationship with the Source of her being...

. . .

Her cell phone was ringing.

"Shaun," she said easily, and laughed. "Hi, Christine... Okay, give me a minute. I'm going in the house now..." She started out of her vehicle.

When Shaun entered her eat-in kitchen, she was still on the phone. "If you need directions, Shaun," Christine was saying, "you can use Route Seventy and..."

"All I'll need is the address in Neptune, Christine..."

"Oh yes, you have your navigation thing..."

Shaun laughed. "Yes, Christine, I have my navigation *thing*... —by the way —how many women you said would be attending the Conference?"

"As I told you, around twenty to twenty five. Why?"

"I need to make sure to walk with enough materials for everyone... —so how are you doing my friend?"

"So how are *you*, doing?"

"You know what I'm going to say, Christine..."

Christine laughed. "I know. Extraordinary... —anyway, Shaun, I'm looking forward to seeing you tomorrow...."

"You'll see me and my mom..."

"Great."

To Shaun, Christina Edwards, who owned a day care center in Lakewood, was the most humble and giving person anyone would want to know. They met at a Christian Chamber function at Cherry Hill almost four years ago and became very good friends.

Christina Edwards was an advocate for children's education

and opportunities. In this vein, she had been instrumental in seeing the formation of drill teams of different ages. Participants were as young as five, and they really did not drill, but tap-danced. Through Christina, Shaun had been able to meet a number of individuals, and saw Christina as the ultimate connector of people.

She rested her handbag on the table cluttered with mail, picked up a glass from the wares rack next to the sink, and drew water from the fountain between the kitchen and living room where Mama Kitty, and Pretty Girl slept. She sat in the dining chair closest to the refrigerator and took her shoes off. Mama Kitty stretched on the green carpet, once more depositing gray fur into the carpet... fur that her Mom, home from her live-in job was destined to clean.

CHAPTER 34: 2003
The Maple Shade Story Continues

A SEASON OF CHANGE

That November, I had taken Carlton on a Pre-Paid legal business cruise to Ensenada, Mexico. He had not too long ago arrived in the U.S. and I was happy to have him accompany me. When we returned to Maple Shade, I was all fired up about implementing all the great training, instruction, and direction I received on the cruise.

There was a lot riding on the next few month of the year 2003. It was November and soon it would be Thanksgiving... soon it would be Christmas, and David Allen was scheduled to be my guest at my Maple Shade apartment that December to help expand our team.

I was working full time at Blue Cross while doing my Pre-Paid Legal Services business on a part time basis. My plate was full and my husband's arrival added a new dimension to my life. I was on longer alone and Independent. I was now a practicing wife to Carlton after ten years of being away from him. Our long-distance relationship was over. After being accustomed to being alone —independent for so long —doing everything more or less for myself for so long, I now had to re-adjust to being one, so to speak, with Carlton. I loved my husband and was determined to do whatever it took to make him comfortable and at home.

Carlton and I, as a husband-and-wife Pre-paid legal Service entity, began to attend group meetings and business functions. He met our PPLSI team, my friends, business associates, and colleagues at Blue Cross. Everyone tried to make him feel accepted.

Thanksgiving came, my first with Carlton, and we were invited to spend the day at my Aunt Desiree and her family in East Orange. At that time my dad was still here recovering from his illness. So

Carlton and I headed North Jersey to spend the holiday with family and visit a few friends he had not seen since the wedding in 2000. We spent some time with Bindhu and her family in Kearney, and spent some time with the Hendersons. Though Carlton was not very hot on socializing—he would have preferred that the two of us simply staying at home and enjoying each other—it was a great day.

Then slowly but surely things between us began to change. It began to be evident that we were two very different people. I guess that we hadn't been together for so long, we had grown apart. But we both wanted our marital relationship to work and were determined to make compromises. There was, however, a lot we had to address to smooth things out, and my Blue Cross work schedule did not make it easy. Normally I'd get into the office for 5: A.M. and leave at 8: P.M. Carlton at that time was not yet working and his long stretches of being alone all day in the apartment bothered me. He endured six months of this since it took him that long to find a job. Of course I knew I was on-path to making my American Dream of owning our own home a reality, but at what cost? My relationship with my husband was most important to me, and what he was going through troubled me deeply. I prayed that he found a job, and I prayed that my Pre-Paid Legal endeavors did not jeopardize our marriage. Things seemed so fragile with us... —so tentative.

. . .

PPLSI Executive Director, David Allen arrived in November and I was ready to run with the agenda we had planned. We had several day and evening appointments, private business receptions and Team training sessions. The highlight of his visit was the business Breakfast at the Hampton Inn. All preparations were made for the function: a continental breakfast was prepared and the room was laid out in a classroom style to accommodate about twenty-five guests. Carlton accompanied me as my co-associate and husband.

The Breakfast was scheduled to begin at 8: A.M. David Allen tested all the equipment to make sure that everything was working. Time slipped by. Now it was 8:10 A.M. and, other than

Tammy Grove, a newfound friend, and businesswoman that I respected, no one else arrived. Out of respect for Tammy's time, David began his presentation to her. David was just a few slides into his Pre-Paid Legal Services presentation, and Tammy had already grasped the value of it. She felt blown away. "Is this for real?" she whispered to me, and added: "I'm signing up. This is a no-brainer; I can do this."

Tammy got the PPLSI membership and became an Independent Associate. She was the only guest, but in my heart I felt that it was worth it.

We had a few more appointments that day which included a State Chamber networking event. Following that, Carlton came along with David Allen and myself to a party held by the local Chamber, after the State Chamber function. This was a night to meet and mingle and dance and have a good time.

David moved around quite comfortably. Soon there was dancing, and David was having a ball on the floor with Tammy. Carlton asked me if I wanted to dance, but I wasn't feeling well. My tummy was beginning to pain and nausea was creeping up on me. The night was still young, so to speak, but I felt tired. I knew that I wanted to go home. Leaving, however, would mean that David's night at the party would be over since I was the driver, and he was staying at my apartment. He was having such a good time and I didn't want to ruin it. I knew that Carlton would not have minded leaving; he seemed very uncomfortable, and wasn't saying much that evening.

At last dinner was served and in my discomfiture, I picked at my food. Somehow I had no appetite. I must not have been looking right to Tammy. She turned to me and asked if I was okay. "I'm fine, Tammy," I said. "What about you?"

She gave me the thumbs up, but she kept looking me right in the eyes and maybe saw the truth of my pain. Carlton saw it too.

"You don't look too good, babes," he said.

I took a deep breath hoping to feel better.

"I don't think Shaun's feeling good," he said to David.

"She doesn't look too good," agreed Tammy.

"I think it's time we take you home, Shaun," David said.

"But David," I said. But they would have none of it.

"No! We're going to leave," David insisted.

I was glad he said that for I felt like I wanted to vomit.

We said our good-byes to the folks at our table; Tammy and I embraced, and we promised to stay in touch.

I drove home in mostly silence.

I went to bed that night hoping that by morning I would be better since David was headed back to California and I had to get him to the airport. The next morning I awoke with a slight pain on my lower Right side.

"What is it, Babes?" Carlton asked. "What's going on?"

I shook my head. I didn't know.

"I think you should rest some more..."

"Doods... I can't. I have to get David to the airport..."

And I did, with lots of time to spare. I thanked David for all his help and patience, drove back home, and got into bed. I was off work for a few days.

CHAPTER 35: 2003
The Maple Shade Story Continues

LAST MISCARRIAGE

The pain in my tummy persisted and I called Dr. O, my Primary Care Physician, and made an appointment. Carlton and I went in to see him. He had some tests run and the results said that I was pregnant. My doctor advised that I see my gynecologist, so I called and got on her scheduled the next day. I arrived at her Office only to be told she was no longer practicing Obstetrics due to an issue with malpractice insurance in New Jersey. She recommended I see one of her partners. "I'm going to brief him on your case, Shaun," she said.

Her associate saw me that very day, but it turned out to be an experience I do not want to remember. After lying on the examination table, the man proceeded to probe me roughly. It seemed like he just wanted to get it done with as quickly as possible. Immediately after he said to me, "You can sit up now..."

I said, "So Doctor, will everything be okay?"

"Your numbers are up," he said. "You *are* pregnant... —however! ...However, I do not think you should be saying anything to anyone just yet..."

"Why is that, doctor?" I asked.

"For starters," he said. "It doesn't look good at all..."

"What do you mean?"

"I have not found anything in your uterus," he said quite casually. "But you can feel free to check back in two weeks —though I doubt there will be any change." And he turned and left the room.

I was dumb founded. This was my seventh pregnancy after six miscarriages... and a doctor who didn't seem to care had coldly dashed the hope for this seventh child. Tears welled up as I got dressed still in pain —some of it due to the way he examined me as though I was an animal. I left that facility hurt and angry. *Why? Why did he treat me like that?*

That night I was still in pain; I could not sleep, and Carlton tried his best to comfort me. "Doods..." I told him, "I can't bear this..."

"You want to go to the hospital?"

"Yes... yes... I have to go..."

"But you'll be able to drive in this pain?"

"I have to, Doods..."

It was about 10: P.M. that I drove with him to the Virtua Hospital emergency room in Voorhees, and had to wait for hours. It was early the following morning that a doctor finally looked at me. They took blood, did an Ultra-sound, found nothing amiss, gave me a few pain relievers, and sent me home.

When morning came I called my Primary Care physician and told him what was happening. He recommended that I call Dr. H with Phoenix Obgyn and get an appointment right away. I did so and she agreed to see me. At that time Carlton did not have his driver's license so I drove in pain to the appointment. He was with me, but how much could he do but hold my free hand.

I arrived at the doctor's office, they signed me in, and she saw me immediately. She asked me what the problem was and I told her —told her everything —including the way I had been treated by the other doctor. She was appalled and surprised as such behavior. She examined me via intra-virginal ultrasound and said, "Mrs. Stephenson... there is something here... but I need to send you to radiology immediately... How will you get there?"

"I'll have to drive, Doctor," I said to her.

"Drive? —In your condition?"

"I'll make it, Doctor," I said grimacing in pain.

"Take care, Mrs. Stephenson... they'll be expecting you."

I left her office slowly and Carlton assisted me back to the car. It was painful to see how helpless he looked. "It's okay," I whispered to him. "Just help me behind the wheel."

In the fifteen to twenty minute drive to radiology, I tried not to think about the pain. When we got there, a technician was waiting. "Mrs. Stephenson?"

I recognized her from the other office where I normally visited for ultra-sound procedures. She knew who I was, because of that

I felt a little relieved. "Mrs. Stephenson... I'll do my best to make you comfortable, okay?"

"Thank you," I said, and the examination began.

"My right side is very painful..." I told her.

"Does it feel tender?" she asked.

"Yes," I whispered in pain.

She directed the probe to that area and made several exposures. Within a few minutes she was done. "Mrs. Stephenson..."

"Call me Shaun," I told her.

"Shaun," she said. "I'm so sorry to hear all that you're going through, but rest a bit. I have to get these readings to the doctor right away, okay?"

"Okay..."

She squeezed my hand and left quickly. *What is it?* I thought. *Oh God! —What is it?*

I took my time, got dressed and waited. Not too long after the doctor came in. He took a deep breath and sat before me with the radiological readings in his hands.

"Mrs. Stephenson," he began, "but I do not want you to get nervous..."

"What is it Doctor?" I asked expecting the worst. "Is it serious?"

He nodded. "It is serious. This is what is known as an ectopic pregnancy —meaning a pregnancy where the embryo is in an abnormal place..." He sighed and continued. "We found a beating heart... —You will need to have an operation —an emergency operation and Dr. H will perform it. You need to get to the Virtua Hospital Emergency room right now. It's that urgent."

I broke down. I could not hold back the tears.

"Is there someone here with you, Mrs. Stephenson?

"My husband is outside..."

So they spoke to Carlton and he tried to be calm but I saw how nervous and scared he was.

The pain was unrelenting, but I pulled myself together. We started off for the hospital, got lost a couple of times, but eventually found it. As soon as I got there I was prepped and taken to the theater for emergency surgery. Dr. H showed up with a smile. She looked at me and held my hand. "Don't you worry, Shaun," she whispered. "We'll take care of you you'll be fine..."

At that moment I knew she meant what she said. I closed my eyes and silently prayed. I held Carlton's hand. I felt his worry. "Pray for me too, Doods… pray for me and you'll see me again."

This was to be the first surgery I would have had in all my thirty-four years, but somehow I was not scared. As I was prepped with IV for anesthesia, I held Dr. H's hand. "Please take care…"

. . .

When I awoke the surgery was over. I was in the recovery room and Carlton stood by my bedside. He told me that he loved me and how good it was to have me back. I was able to give a weak smile, but I felt woozy.

I felt my tummy and it was taped from side to side. Dr. H visited me and explained what they had done in the theater. She explained that they had to do major surgery due to the enlarged fibroids they discovered inside of me and as such could not get to my right tube by laparoscopy. So they made a cesarean cut. As for the fibroids, they did not take them out because I had not given them consent to.

I was also told that my right fallopian tube had to be removed because the fetus was lodged inside of it. Later, however, I learnt from reading the pathology notes, that such was not the case —that it was not necessary to have taken out the tube —that the fetus was not lodged inside of it but outside of it and in the abdominal cavity. I was not prepared to sue anyone, however. Dr. H had saved my life and I was on the road to recovery.

Later, I was taken to a room where I would spend next three days. I didn't know what Carlton was going to do. He couldn't drive my car back to Maple Shade, so he was stranded at the hospital. He stayed with me the duration, making out the best way he could.

After I was discharged, two of my friends from Blue Cross came to take us home. One drove Carlton and I, while the other followed in my vehicle.

I was on disability for six weeks. I could not drive for almost one month. It was a challenging recovery. Carlton tried to cook and clean. He did the best he could. My Pre-Paid Legal Services business was on hold and soon Christmas, and the New Year was going to soon be with us.

CHAPTER 36: 2003

The Maple Shade Story Continues

COMING TO GRIPS WITH DISABILITY

She turned very carefully in bed, adjusted her pillow, and gazed past a wintry bough that jutted past the two large windows. The sound of the morning traffic was muted. In her six years at Horizon Blue Cross Blue Shield of New Jersey, Shaun Stephenson, a proverbial Energizer bunny, had never been on disability. Between her three-day stay at the hospital and her now being at home, she had come to terms with her very limited mobility.

She wished her mom was there to help Carlton take care of her, but her mom just couldn't be there. Shaun was the one that drove to pick her mom up from train station. She had to be content with talking to her mom on the phone.

She felt the need to go to the bathroom and was glad that Carlton was not around to fuss around her —to treat her like someone physically challenged. She was going to get there by herself —she wanted, so much, to be able to go to the bathroom on her own.

She used her elbows and managed to sit up. It was difficult because of the stiffness she felt about her tummy that was puffy and tender and taped above where the internal stitches were. Breathing carefully, she got her legs over the side of the bed and onto the floor. She leaned forward, and with her arms, began pushing herself to her feet. Her arms trembled slightly, but at last she was standing.

I can do this...

Slowly she started for the bathroom not far away.

When she got back from the bedroom, she turned carefully and sat on the edge of the bed. She gazed somewhat blankly at the carpeted floor. She was thinking back to a few days before the Cherry Hill Chamber party. She had been a virtual dynamo —on fire! —she was going to be the Joan of Arc of Pre-Paid Legal

Services in South Jersey! Little did she know that within a week of that festive event after the Cherry Hill networking event she would have been literally flat on her back. She smiled weakly and shook her head slowly...

Life is so fragile...

Shaun Stephenson thought of fate... of how many people's lives were now intertwined with hers... the nurse at the emergency room... the doctor at the radiology unit... Doctor H who surely had saved her life. She sighed deeply and her eyes were closed once again in a prayer of thanks... a prayer of gratitude. The operation was her second time facing death, the first time being the accident... *For what reason, Lord? Why am I living today, Lord? What is my mission?*

She thought of Carlton. He was in the kitchen. He was singing a calypso to himself as he prepared breakfast for her. Within only three months of his being in America so many things had happened to her.

Lord? Are you trying to tell me something?

Is it something that I'm not doing?

Is it something that I need to do —to do better?

Are you punishing me for something, Lord?

She twisted herself carefully, drew her legs back onto the bed, and lay down once more. She gazed thoughtfully at the huge arrangement of flowers her Blue Cross co-workers had sent her. Carlton was singing a new Calypso, this time about the drunken man in a graveyard. She closed her eyes and smiled. He was happy to have her all to himself.

It was not that she didn't like being alone with her husband, but she felt driven. There was so much she wanted for her family. Above all she was going to buy herself a home. Only death would stop her. She was tired of moving from apartment to apartment; from rented townhouse to rented townhouse —tired of the nomadic life. To own her own home to which her tired mother can come home, was her primary focus, hence the hours she worked at Blue Cross, hence her commitment to making good as a Pre-Paid Legal Services Independent Associate... hence the missteps.

She thought of the Hilton Hotel failure... she thought of the Business breakfast flop... "Those were just that: missteps... —lessons..." She sighed. "I'll do better next time. I just *have* to stop assuming so much... I just have to force myself to see things as they *really* are!"

Carlton came into the bedroom. "Babes..." he said, carefully balancing a covered tray. "I have something here for you..."

"Help me sit up, Doods..." she said.

CHAPTER 37: 2003·2004
The Maple Shade Story Continues

A PAINFUL LIMBO

I was not yet out of the woods, however; the fibroids they discover were enlarged and a decision had to be made soon. Dr. H recommended I see an infertility specialist for further tests and procedures.

As long as I could remember I suffered with painful periods and tummy pain. After this, my seventh miscarriage that led to surgery, it dawned on me that I had gone through years of doctors and specialists probing into me and running tests to no avail. No definitive answers.

I first found out I had fibroids back in 1998; they were just the size of pebbles. Due to earlier pregnancies and miscarriages over the years, however, they became enlarged. At this point in my life I was simply tired —fed up with visiting doctors.

Carlton saw and felt my frustration and he did his best to comfort me. "You're alive, Babes," he said to me one night. "And where there's life there's hope... You're getting better... Let's take it one day at a time..."

The irony of it all was that we had been apart for so long and now on the start of our life together sickness seemed to be my lot. I was tired of being laid up at home for six weeks. It came with a feeling of helplessness that was acute. Carlton was not yet working and we had had a little left on our savings. I regretted being at home. I *was* getting my regular pay, but funds were low. Had I been at work I would have been making overtime in order to be on top of the bills. Things for us grew even more challenging after the apartment management raised the rent for the new year.

I was scheduled to return to work in January 2004, but was still very weak and stayed at home for an extra two weeks. So, being off for two months, our rent was late for that month. I returned to work but could not do the long hours because I was still recovering. If I tried to push myself I got tired and felt dizzy.

Things were a little better between Carlton and me because I was home before nightfall, and did not leave home early in the mornings as I did before I fell ill. But financially, we were struggling. There was a promotion and a raise that was pending for me, but I didn't know when it was going to come. I was hoping and praying.

And then Carlton told me about the phone call he had received from an ex client who wanted him to return to Guyana and execute a graphics project. "I'm going to do it," he said. "The guy is going to pay me in U.S. dollars —and you *know* we can use it, Shaun!"

While he was away I began to push myself on the job once again. I was much stronger now and was eager to resume my early-morning to late-night Blue Cross schedule. Pure determination and a desire to succeed, kept me going. One day before Carlton's return, I was able to restart old schedule of 5: A.M. to 8: P.M. It felt good to be back.

Time flew and Carlton was scheduled back. That weekend I drove to New York to pick him up from JFK. When he finally emerged I hugged him tightly... ever so tightly. It was strange how much I had missed him. I missed him like I never did before. Maybe it was because of our togetherness before and after my surgery. I guess I had found a new appreciation for life *and* the man in my life... a man who trusted me so much —a man to whom I was his everything.

As we drove home and he told me that it had been 'okay' being back in Guyana...

"Just okay?"

"Yeah," he said with a whimsical sneer. "It wasn't all that..."

"Why?"

"I missed you too much, Babes," he said and reached for my hand. "I missed you so much... I don't think I can be away from you... —ever again..."

. . .

The following week I had my first appointment with a specialist, to discuss my fibroids. Prior to this visit Carlton and I had a spoke about starting our own family.

"Maybe after the fibroids you'll be able to make a baby, Babes," he said. "We're together now... This is the best time for us to start our family..."

"But Doods..."

"Sssh! ... You have to stop thinking you'll lose them all, Babes..."

"Okay..."

But I was tired of it all.

"We have to pray about this, Babes... and I know that one day God will give us a baby... You'll see this specialist guy; he'll get rid of the fibroids, and you'll be able to make a baby..."

.   .   .

I saw the specialist, he thought I should have surgery, but I did not care to go through another. So I began to do my own research on the best remedies for fibroids, and told Margie Henderson about it. She too felt I should not subject myself to yet another surgery. "A lot of times these doctors don't know what they're doing," she said. "Believe me, Shaun. A lot of times they botch things up and you know who suffers?"

"But I don't know what to do now, Marge..."

"Listen, Shaun! I'm going to give you the name of a great doctor you should see! —He's the best in the field of saving women's uterus!"

She gave me the name of one Dr. G in Manhattan, New York, and then told me the story of a woman who saw him after all her previous doctors had had told her she needed to have a hysterectomy because her fibroids were so bad. Dr. G did laser surgery on her, and a few months later she was pregnant with her miracle child.

The story Marge told, gave me hope.

I called Dr. G's office, spoke to the receptionist, and was told that I would have to wait three months to see him. I was advised to come prepared with all my medical notes and x-rays. But that appointment was some three months away, and between making that call and the appointment in New York, so much transpired in my life...

. . .

It was now 2004 and I had started back on the old grind at Blue Cross. I felt back to my old self. Carlton, though, was not happy because of it. He felt, I guess, as if in sickness we were together, but once I was back on my feet, he ceased to matter. Of course that was so far from the truth.

Because he relied on me to drive him around, he was at a disadvantage. While I was at work there were few places he could have gone to, few job leads he could have exploited, so it was important that acquired his U.S. Driver's License. I spoke to him about it, and got him the Manual to study and prepare for the test. At first he was reluctant, but he did it anyway.

To help him over his anxiety about driving in America I had him drop me to work and pick me up afterwards. At the same time he was trying to get a job in his field as a graphic artist but was having no luck. Financially, things were becoming desperate. At nights he would be up late on the computer sending out resumes and doing his writing. During the day he was merely at home with nothing to do or anywhere to go. He was frustrated with many things and this included my Pre-Paid Legal Service efforts. He no longer wanted to attend PPLSI meetings and functions. He felt that he did not fit in, and my closeness to many of the men in the business made him uncomfortable —emasculated. I guess this feeling was compounded because he had not yet found a job. Whenever the team came over to our apartment for meetings he would stick around to welcome them —to say hello and then retreat upstairs. There he would remain until they were gone. And I knew his continual absence at my home-presentations was not lost on anyone.

I was trying to get back into my Pre-Paid Legal Services endeavors, work at my full time job with Blue Cross, and to take care of my marital relationship. It was a very difficult balancing act. My days were long, and when I got home I still had the responsibility to cook and clean. Carlton was all thumbs in the kitchen. The domestic tension that started to grow between us because of my commitment as a Pre-Paid Legal Services associate bothered me. My relationship with Carlton became fragile.

I realized that my commitment to Blue Cross and my PPLSI endeavors was threatening to destroy my marriage and that I had to let one go. I had to make a choice.

So I threw PPLSI business into the back seat for the next few years, and I concentrated my efforts on my relationship with my husband, my full time job at Blue Cross, and a commitment to buy our own home. At that time, I also began to feel that maybe there was need for God in our lives and felt the need to be part of a church congregation, and began attending The Living Faith Christian Center, in Pennsauken New Jersey. The congregation was over six thousand strong, and Carlton went with me a few times. Soon after he said that he did not want to go any more.

The church experience affected Carlton. It brought back too many painful memories from our church back in Guyana: Many of the other young people in the congregation knew that Carlton and I were together, but did not approve. They felt he was too poor and not right for me. Lots had happened during those years, and Carlton developed resentment for churches across the board. America was not going to change that.

I committed to continue since it had been a long time that I had been searching for a church home. I felt that I needed to be grounded spiritually, and attended in quest of Truth. It helped some, but I felt that there was something that was still missing. So I began an inner search; I began to look within, and stayed under the pastor's teaching for almost three years.

· · ·

After being at home for seven months, Carlton eventually found a job in Delanco City, twenty minutes away. How would we be able to utilize one car between us? Since I was just one mile from work, I opted to let him drive to his work location with me in the car so he can learn the route. Then I would drive to my job and come back for him when his day was done. This meant that we had to be out of the house by 5: A.M. I changed my schedule at my job to facilitate him, and began working from 6: A.M. He learnt the way quickly and was soon comfortable with the traffic.

With him and I working, our financial situation got better,

and we decided that we were going to buy our house in the next year. We began to save seriously —cutting out every unnecessary expense —the cable TV service went. Even our groceries were affected: No more snacks and frivolous stuff like that. In order to maximize my over time hours and make even more money, I started working weekends.

But there was still the necessity for us to get another car since I needed to get back to my old work schedule that generated more overtime pay. Through a friend, we were able to buy a 1990 Nissan Maxima with over two hundred thousand miles, for just one thousand dollars. We spent a little money to fix it, and in the end, it ran well enough. Carlton called her 'Betsy.'

My health challenges still had to be met, however, and my appointment with Dr. G was coming up.

I was prepared.

CHAPTER 38: 2004

The Maple Shade Story Continues

SALUTE TO A CARING SURGEON

We headed to NY to see Dr. G with all my medical records in hand and buoyancy in my heart. Somehow I knew it was going to be a very defining visit. Somehow I felt very optimistic about Dr. G's laser procedure that I had read about on the Internet. I knew he was held in very high esteem for his success rate in corrective surgery to the uterus.

I parked at the Hamilton Train Station and we took a sixty-minute NJ Transit train ride to 34 Street, New York, NY. It was Carlton's first trip by train. I pointed out things to him and he enjoyed the ride. It was also going to be the very first time he was going to be walking the streets of Manhattan.

We got the train at 34th Street, caught a yellow taxi, headed to the upper West Side for 84th and Park Avenue, and arrived with time to spare. I checked in, and waited our turn to see the doctor. There was a lot of reading material on Dr. G. Having created a unique set of laser equipment; he had many successes with his type of surgery. He had also written a book on why hysterectomies are not always necessary. He advocated that a woman has a right to leave the world with all the parts she was born with.

Finally it was our turn and we went in to meet with this illustrious doctor I had been reading about. Dr. G. was a pleasant and cheery man—soft spoken and direct—who looked in his fifties. He was very cordial with us before we settled down to the details of my visit. I guess it was his way to make us feel at ease. In conversation we found out he had a son my age. I told him that we would like to have children but with my current situation it seemed doubtful. He wagged his finger slowly. "No," he said. "There is always hope..."

In a very comfortable room he proceeded to examine me in

a non-invasive way and I couldn't believe it. In my mind I said, "Wow!" Through the entire procedure I felt secure, safe, and dignified. As he did what he did, he spoke to me respectfully, and in my mind I thought, *Here is a doctor who sees me as just another human being.*

In my estimation it took Dr. G less than two minutes to do a quick but specific pelvic exam that left me feeling dignified. He also did an ultra-sound that showed up on the monitor on which Carlton and I could have seen images of my uterus.

Dr. G detailed a few options as it related to my case and then decided on the best and less evasive for me. He explained that my fibroids were intramural —within the walls of the uterus and that the best way to proceed was by reducing them. He explained that I would have to take a prescribed injection once a month, one that would be administered to my hip at the same time every thirty days for three months, a period through which my period would stop. And after ninety days were up, he would perform laser surgery on me.

Three months went by, and before I knew it, November 8th, the date for my surgery arrived, and I was ready.

CHAPTER 39: 2004
The Maple Shade Story Continues

LASER SURGERY

Surgery was scheduled for 9: A.M. and Bindhu got us to the Lennox Hill Hospital in Manhattan with ample time to spare. Carlton, knowing ahead of time that I would have to remain in the hospital for three days, came prepared to stay the duration at the facility. He walked with his books, extra sweatshirts, and a jacket for warmth.

I checked into the Hospital, filled out all documents and was prepped for the procedure. It surprised me that while I was being prepared Dr. G was already there. I had grown used to doctors only showing up just in time to do what they have to do. But he was there making sure that all the necessary paperwork and other details was attended to.

As they were taking me to the waiting room before the theater, Carlton was with me; Dr. G was too. He remained with us until his operating room was ready. It was only then that he left me, and only briefly, to be suited up.

When he returned, he told me that I'd be going into the theater soon. "How are you doing, Mr. Stephenson?" he said to Carlton.

Carlton smiled; it was strained.

"Just think positively, Mr. Stephenson. She'll do well... she'll be well. I'll take care of her..."

I had being lying in the bed with my legs crossed. Dr. G uncrossed them. "I need you to relax, Shaun," he said. "Close your eyes and relax... we are going to take good care of you..."

Then it was time. Carlton kissed me. "See you soon, Babes," he whispered, and I was wheeled into surgery.

. . .

The anesthesiologist found my vein and gave me a smile of reassurance; Dr. G held my hand and said a silent prayer. I prayed also and asked that he be guided and directed by God's hands... and a calm —a peacefulness overcame me...

When I awoke Carlton and Dr. G were giving me the thumbs up. "Everything went excellent, Babes," Carlton said, and I smiled. Doctor G squeezed my shoulder gently. "All you need to do now is rest, Shaun. I'll check on you tomorrow." Then he left Carlton and I alone.

The Doctor had told me the recovery time was going to be less than three weeks, and as I lay there I felt well for just having come out of surgery. The next morning I wanted to go to the bathroom. So I asked the nurse to remove the catheter that was in me. She got the okay from the doctor and she took it out. Then I went to the bathroom by myself.

I spent then next three days just being monitored. It was a distinct difference than the previous surgery. My recovery was rapid. The fibroids were gone. I was finally free of them and my mind was focused on getting better and better and being back at work to continue on the quest for our new home.

During the days Carlton was with me in my private hospital room. At nights, he sat with me as long as he could. He was not permitted to sleep in my room. And after leaving, he would retire to the cafeteria where he slept uncomfortably in whatever chair he found. His luck ran both ways on the second day; first it was bad, then it was good. Someone reported that that there was a strange man who was sleeping in the cafeteria and who had been hanging around the premises for the last two days, and Carlton was pointed out. A security guard approached him. "Sir, I have to do this... Someone reported that you're some kind of trespasser on hospital grounds..."

"I'm not a trespasser, sir..." Carlton said, "but it's just that my wife is here; she had surgery two days ago, and I'm not allowed to stay in her room..."

"So why don't you go home?" the guard asked him.

"We live very far away over in New Jersey," Carlton said, "and I can't go home because I don't know the way. I'm new in the country..."

"Okay," the guard said.

"That's why I slept in the cafeteria..."

"I understand," the guard said. "I guess nobody told you that we have a guest lounge here..."

"No, I didn't know that, sir..."

The guard sympathized with him and showed him the guest lounge. Carlton said that he wished he had known this two days earlier.

That night he was able to sleep in a comfortable easy chair.

· · ·

I was discharged on the morning of the fourth day. Bindhu arrived soon after to pick up Carlton and me. She seemed so happy to see me and to know that everything had gone well. When we got to Bindhu's home where my car was parked, there was a pleasant surprise in store for Carlton and I. Bindhu made sure I had food for the next week. Her husband Sam, who was a chef with a Caribbean flair, made rotis, pot bakes, rice and dhal, curried chicken —you name it. There was quite a bit of food.

Then we were ready to leave.

"Who's going to drive, Shaun? —You can't drive, you know," Bindhu said, and Carlton spoke up.

"I'm going to drive," he said.

It was a relief to be going home to my apartment and my bed. We got home before night fell and Carlton was totally relieved as well.

Thanksgiving was nearing but all we planned to do was stay home and be together. This was our first anniversary and his second Christmas in America. It was my second back-to-back surgery —the last taking place one year ago around the same time. There was a lot to be grateful for and I thanked God for Life and another chance to make my contribution to life.

My recovery was remarkable. I was able to drive in less than one week, and one week after I had been discharged I had a scheduled follow-up visit with Dr. G. He was pleased to see how well I was recovering. He explained to me what he had done. He told me what had turned up during, my surgery—called a mayo-ectomy— were eight mayomas of differing sizes. He also told me that there were scar tissue that were attached to the walls of my small intestines, and to remove them, it had been necessary to lift the uterus out, and repair the lining.

He did an examination and was pleased with the size and shape of the Uterus. Things were progressing well. I visited him once a month, for the next six months, and on my last visit he recommended that I saw a specialist for In-Vitro fertilization.

CHAPTER 40: 2005

The Maple Shade Story Continues

IN-VITRO FERTILIZATION OR IVF

The process of IVF is made up of many steps. First, the ovaries are shut down temporarily using a drug called Lupron, which must be taken for two weeks prior to the procedure. Next, The ovaries are stimulated using a series of ten-day injections of a drug called Pergonal. Then, when the eggs are ready for harvesting, the woman is given hCG to induce final maturation, and then the eggs are harvested by the process of Ultrasound Guided Vaginal Retrieval. In this process the patient is heavily sedated, a thin needle is passed into the ovaries, and the eggs are suctioned from the follicles (5-15 eggs being collected). Each egg is then fertilized with about 100,000 motile sperm. If the sperm do not fertilize the eggs themselves, an Intracytoplasmic Sperm Injection (ICSI) is then to puncture the egg and inject a sperm into it.

Following the retrieval, the embryos are observed for 3-6 days. During this time, if the goal of IVF is to prevent the fetus from inheriting the gene his or her parent may have, then eggs or sperm (whichever the parent may possess) are tested for the gene. They are then selected and the procedure being the same whether or not this is a factor, next, about three to four embryos are then selected and placed in a catheter and transferred through the cervix into the uterus. After two weeks a pregnancy test can be obtained, and after four weeks the fetal heartbeat can be observed by ultrasound.

. . .

I made an appointment to see a fertility specialist at Penn University. His name was Dr. C. He had been recommended as one of the best, and so Carlton and I made our very first visit to his practice. When we got there, he had not come in as yet. One of his staff, however, showed us into his office where we sat to await his arrival.

He arrived soon after and there was a female with him. "The Stephenson's," he said. "We're so glad you're here..."

"We are too," I said.

He introduced the woman with him as one of his interns whom he had asked to sit in. "Because your case is so unique, Mrs. Stephenson," he said. "I invited her to sit in on this consultation. Do you mind?"

Carlton and I didn't mind.

They sat, and he began to speak with us lightly —I guess to break the ice. I felt very comfortable with him.

At last he said, "I have already gone over an evaluation of your case that was sent to me..."

And then the consultation began. It was a very intense one. As we got into the specifics of my medical records, he was obviously amazed at what he had gathered from it. And when he listened to me, he was impressed by all the research I had done.

He began to detail our options as it related to my many miscarriages and the fact that I had only my left fallopian tube. "The in-vitro fertilization process," he said to us. "Is a recourse I would recommend."

"My wife making a baby like this..." Carlton began. "Would it be what they term a 'test tube' baby, doctor?"

Dr. C nodded. "You're correct, Mr. Stephenson... —Yes, when people speak about test-tube babies, they are speaking about a baby being conceived through the In-Vitro fertilization process..." And then he launched into explaining the process to us.

"Are there any assurances that it will work?" Carlton asked.

"There are no guarantees, Mr. Stephenson. In every situation like this we hope the process works for the sake of couples like yourself and wife here. It's a tough fact..."

"We understand, Doctor," I said.

To me he fidgeted a bit in his chair before he said, "If that fails—and this is so difficult to say because I understand—there is always the option of adoption..."

"Doctor," I said. "We need some time to think through all that you've told us..."

"By all means, Shaun!" Dr. C said effusively. "This is all up to you and your husband, and I'm here to give you any help you may need in coming to whatever decision. Call me if you need to. Just know that if you decide to go along with the IVF procedure my team will do all they can to make you comfortable. You would be assigned a nurse specifically for the duration."

At last the consultation ended. We thanked Dr. C for his patience and compassion. We again told him that we were going to consider all that he had told us and get back to him with a decision. We said our good byes and started back for New Jersey. We were both off of work that day.

· · ·

The drive home was mainly silent. I guess we both had a lot to contemplate. I was thinking about the IVF process and the time I'd have to take off work to go to PA each day. I would lose my overtime. It was giving me a ton of things to think about since Carlton and I were then in the middle for saving for our home. It was going to happen; we were going to start signing the paperwork soon. I was seriously conflicted. *Should we press on with buying our house now, or should concentrate on trying to get that baby that has eluded us for so many years?*

Then is as if Carlton had been reading my thoughts, he broke his silence and said, "It's up to you, Babes... this is your choice as to if you want to, or when you want us to try this In-Vitro thing... It's up to you..."

"I'll need time to figure out what I want to do, Carlton..."

He nodded. "I understand..."

We drove the rest of the way in silence.

It took me a few days to even get back to the subject of Dr. C.

We went back to work as usual the next day.

Carlton would always call me on my job at lunchtime to see how I was doing, and we would talk for a few minutes. When he called the day after we had seen Dr. C, I felt as though I needed to be with him as early as I could, and did not work late that day. I felt I needed to be home early with my husband due to the past days event.

He was surprised and happy to see me home early. We had

a night of home movies; we grew up liking movies. So cuddling in bed that night brought back a lot of old memories. We reminisced about how far we had come... about how great it felt to be together again after so many years of separation... no more long phone calls... no more emails...

I remember Carlton's body warm against mine...

It felt great.

CHAPTER 41: 2005
The Maple Shade Story Continues

AN AMERICAN DREAM: HOME OWNERSHIP

There were a few things I had to take care of before committing to In-Vitro Fertilization. Carlton, my mom, and I were determined to own our own house.

As Carlton came home from work that very afternoon, it so happened that the Health Channel was on. It had become my favorite channel to watch. It was where I saw stories about women who made children despite the odds.

He said to me, "Babes, you should ease watching these shows, you know. They would only stress you out about your situation..."

"Speaking about that," I said. "I think I've made my decision about that In-Vitro Fertilization thing..."

"Oh yeah?"

"Yes... I'm going to postpone trying to make a baby for a while..."

When I weighed all the things pending: A visit by Carlton's mom and sister, and then there was my dad. Within a few months he would be picking up his Resident Alien visa to travel to America. It was clear to me that the purchase of the home was vital, and that we should to wait another year before we moved forward on trying for the baby. I shared my thoughts with him.

Carlton said that he understood and agreed —that it indeed made sense to wait until 2006 to go ahead with plans for a Child. I was happy to get that off my chest for a while.

And my long days at work continued.

. . .

I had begun talks with Monica McGill regarding the purchase of a home. She wore a few hats. Monica was a Real Estate Agent as well as a mortgage consultant with First Interstate Bank, and hoped to have me pre-qualified for a mortgage with them.

Monica had pulled my credit and began to track expenses that needed to be kept up to date, and to inform me of things that had to be done to close the process. My Credit Score was moving in the right direction, so she set out to find those mortgage programs that facilitated individuals in my bracket. She was determined to find the best one for me and had begun shopping for a suitable program, and had found one.

So, as 2005 rolled in, Carlton, my mom, and me just needed a few more months to save enough. We thought we were well on our way to owning our own home.

We began looking at homes as the winter broke in Feb of 2005. Monica took us to see homes she had pulled up and identified as potential. I wanted some place no more than thirty minutes away from my Blue Cross job. At that time my Maple Shade apartment was less than five minutes away. For me, buying a house too far away was not going to be too wise a move unless the price was worth it.

We looked into cities and counties neighboring Maple Shade. There was Cherry Hill, Voorhees, Burlington, Atco, Pennsauken, and others. But it seemed every property that we liked was either gone or under contract.

March and April went by without a choice. Then we found a house in Pennsauken for an Ok sort of price, but it wasn't right for Carlton. He felt the neighbors were too close for comfort and there was too little land space to the property. He came from a background where his mom owned several acres; so coming to America did not change his ambition of land ownership. I, on the other hand, just wanted us to have a place to call our own and would have settled for the Pennsauken property. I agreed to pass on it, however. I was, however, becoming a little frustrated that things were not moving as quickly. We seemed not to be finding that house we all could have settled for.

I spoke to God one night in prayer. I said, "God... I am tired of this search and need help! Please! ...Please direct Monica to the home that's right for us..."

In my mind it had to have at least four bedrooms to accommodate both of our relatives coming to visit us in America.

A few days later I went online and began doing some searches. This time I began looking further south of where we were —to Woodbury, West Deptford, Glassboro and such. I came upon a few but one stood out, and it was in a place named Mantua.

I looked up the location on Map Quest, and decided that I'd take off from work and go find this place. Strange, even though I had only seen the picture of the house, in my mind I felt this was going to be my home —that this was it!

That day I took off from work at lunchtime and went to find 433 Berkley Road in a place named Mantua. I traveled on Route 295 South about twelve miles before exiting at Exit 23B and unto 45 South. I got to a gas station at Elm Street and then turned back thinking I must have by-passed my destination. As I got back into Woodbury I stopped at another gas station, saw an elderly gentle-man coming towards me, and asked him how for directions to Berkley Rd.

"You did not go far enough, my dear," he said. "Just go back up the street and you'll see a shopping center. Go past that and you'll see a Walgreens pharmacy. Make a right turn there. That's Berkley Road."

I thanked him and retraced my route, saw the Walgreens Pharmacy, and made the turn onto Berkley. I drove along the quiet street that felt like a long country road. I missed the house, made a U-turn, drove back, and made a right turn into its the driveway and pebbled parking area. I found it.

It was an extended ranch that sat back from the street. The size of it was perfect. The yard was spacious. There was a wrap-around deck and right away I knew Doods and my Mom would like it. I fell in love with the house instantly.

I was so pleased and excited with this find that I called Monica immediately, gave her the location and details, and asked that she get the permission for us to see the interior of it that very evening. I guess she felt my enthusiasm and assured me that she would get in touch with the listing agent immediately and then get back to me.

I headed back to work on a cloud and kept all my doings to myself. When Carlton got home that afternoon, he called me and I told him the good news.

Monica had gotten permission for us to see the house, so that evening I picked up Carlton, and drove to Mantua with Monica following in her car.

As we drove, I told Carlton a little more about the house from online details I had printed. He seemed happy about the prospects but did not say too much. Inside, I was praying that he too liked it, since for me this *was* it.

When we got there Monica opened the front door and we entered the living room. It was well lit and simply decorated. There were two bedrooms on the first floor a kitchen to the right, an extra room than let out to an enclosed three-seasons porch that led to the warp around deck. It was dark so we could not see much of the yard, but it was spacious enough.

"Yes!" Carlton said and I laughed in my heart.

Upstairs of it were two bedrooms, a bath and closets.

The kitchen was small; I didn't like the wallpaper; but all in all I thought it was a great find.

The bonus for Carlton was the Basement. Although it was unfinished there was a lot of extra space with a ton of possibilities.

"I like it, babes! I like it!" Carlton said excitedly, and I breathed a sigh of relief.

The thought in my head then, was, *How much?* and, *Can we afford it?*

I looked at Monica. "What do you think?" I asked her.

"I like it."

"Can you put in a bid for me as soon as possible?"

She nodded smiling. "Wow... You really like it, your husband too. I'll do that."

I called my Mom and told her the great news.

We made an offer the next day and the paperwork began. We had to put down three thousand dollars for the commitment contract. My mom provided this from her savings, the homeowner agreed, and the process was on the way.

Monica secured the mortgage commitment approval letter and all the other necessary documentation. By then my Credit score was on target. Everything began to come together in a smooth way.

At last I met the owner and he was pleasant. He welcomed me in give me a tour showing me all the details that Carlton and I had missed in our excitement.

A closing date was set, papers were signed, and Yippie! We did final walk through that day and collected the keys to our new home.

. . .

Carlton and I stood on the porch of our newly bought Mantua, New Jersey home... He hugged me closed to him and said nothing out loud though I heard his joy clearly.

"This is your dream, babes," he said at last.

"Couldn't have done it without you, Doods..."

He chuckled as he gazed past the pair of yard sheds towards the swimming pool at the back of our expansive yard.

"A penny for your thoughts," I said.

He said, "A pool... wow..." and shook his head in the apparent wonder of it. "We have a house with a swimming pool... —wow!" He nodded. "Great land space too." He looked at me. "You know what I'm going to do?"

"What?"

"You know... I'm, going to plant a big garden at the back there, Babes... —huge! It's going to be huge! What's the best season to start planting stuff here?"

. . .

One week after we had closed on the Mantua house, Carlton's Mom and Sister arrive in America for a six-month vacation. They arrived in last month on our lease at the Maple Shade apartment. That we were soon going to be owners of a house was a pleasant surprise for them. They eagerly shared the excitement of moving and pitched in with the packing in preparation for moving that had been scheduled for June 12, 2005. Everything was on target.

"What are you thinking?" Carlton asked me as we stood on the deck of our new home.

"That before we move *anything* in, I want to have prayers and an anointment throughout the house..."

"True... we must thank God. Who we're going to ask to do it for us?"

"I'll call my aunt Desiree and ask her..."

I called her and she agreed. One day before we made the move from Maple Shade, all of us—my in-laws, my Mom, my aunt and me—spent the day in Mantua.

Aunt Desiree led us all in prayer before we began the process of 'cleaning out' the house, and I would always remember my private prayer that day. I prayed in gratitude to God for the many blessings, and I gave thanks for the health and strength that had gotten us to that point of achievement. In my prayer I acknowledged the support of my Mom and husband. I asked that harmony and peace to be the order of our lives in that house —that there be no confusion and that our move from Maple Shade to Mantua be smooth as everything concerning the house had been thus far. I prayed for happiness and contentment in the heart of our family and relatives... I prayed for continued health to take care of and upkeep our new home... I prayed for the strength to remain humble and to be thankful in all things... I prayed that our new home forever be open to those in need. And I gave all praises to God —the one Source of all good things.

After that, we went into each room with blessed olive oil that was touched upon each door and sprinkled into corners as we prayed for good fortune and the exorcism of all lingering negative forces. Again I prayed privately —asking that whatever Forces not of God that may still be dwelling in the house be removed and cast out. I prayed for lightness and free air in my home.

For me it was an emotional experience. I was now thirty-five years old, and at last... my days of being a nomadic renter were over. I was a homeowner after some twelve challenging years in America. I had moved from bankruptcy to what many consider the realization of an American Dream: Home ownership. I could not stop the tears and my family wept with me. Joyce, my mother-in-law hugged me. In tears she reminded me of a promise I had made to her before I left Guyana... that one day she would be able to come to America and be comfortable in a home owned by Carlton and me, and here she was —happy and overjoyed.

· · ·

June 12th, 2005, almost summer. My Mom had her own room with an adjoining bath, on the first floor. Joyce, my mother-in-law and her daughter shared the other bedroom on the same floor. They utilized the bathroom that adjoined my Mom's room. Upstairs, Carlton and I had the master bedroom. He and I used the other bedroom on that floor as an office.

It was really great to have family around. That had always been a desire of mine: to be able to have relatives over at my home where they would be truly comfortable and where they could stay as long as they wanted.

Summer was just around the corner, and Harry from whom the house was bought, came over and helped 'open' the pool.

Everything was coming together.

CHAPTER 42: 2005
The Mantua Story Continues

THE HEART TO CARE... THE WILLINGNESS TO SERVE

2005. It was the Saturday before father's day and she and her mom headed to the JFK Airport. They were going to pick up her Dad. He had finally retired from his job back in Guyana with the Telephone Company after thirty-five years, and was finally coming to America to begin a new life with his family. He was going to be landing, finally, as a U.S. resident. She was hoping that he could settle-in and, in a few years, help her other brothers and sister come to America. That was so much her heart's desire.

It was going to be his first time back since his sickness in 2003 and Shaun was excited to see how he looked. She was eager to see how he had fared health-wise.

At last the plane landed, and the wait to see him emerge into 'arrivals' began. She and her mom waited patiently for him to clear immigration. After what seemed a lifetime, her father, tall and handsome was coming. He stood out of the crowd. Her mom, beside herself, began to wave to catch his attention. He spotted them and broke out smiling.

He hugged Shaun and then turned, laughing, to his wife, and they embraced.

It was a special joy to see my mom and dad hugged together. A lot had had gone on between them for years, but my mother, the ever-faithful wife, loved my dad with all her being. As my dad hugged mom, I could have seen the joy in her... and I wondered what she was probably thinking. Was she telling herself that, finally, she had him for herself?

Throughout her life with him back home, my dad was a literal 'playboy' and my mom had to be content with sharing him with a bevy of local women that he had. I guess my mother was thinking that he was now in America —a new country... I guess she was

189

optimistic of a new beginning for him and her. And in my mind I prayed it would be that way.

On the way home the atmosphere in the car was very light; we chitchatted about this and that, and then he said, "What's the name of the place we're going to now? —Don't tell me. Let me see if I can remember the name... " He squeezed his eyes shut playfully and then shortly after blurted, "Maple Leaf!"

My mom laughed. "You're close to the name of that place, but that's not where we're going..."

"What you mean?" my dad said.

She looked at me and laughed.

"Dad," I said. "We have a big surprise for you..."

"So what the place name? —Is not Maple Leaf?"

"Maple Shade," I corrected.

"Maple Shade, yes! That's it!"

"But that's not where we're going, dad... That is where I used to rent an apartment..."

"What your daughter is trying to tell you," mom said, "is that she bought her own house..."

"What?" her Dad shouted above the hum of the highway traffic. "Shaun buy her own house?"

"That was the surprise I had for you, Dad..."

"Yes," Mom said, and told him how we had only moved in a week ago and that she had furnished her room with new furniture in anticipation of his coming. She wanted him to feel at home and comfortable. My hope was that he allowed himself to settle into a new life —a new life of direction in America.

"You bought your own house..." He nodded. "Congrats my daughter."

He seemed sincere and didn't say very much after that. He looked tired from the flight and soon leaned his head onto my mom mother's shoulder and slept most of the two-hour drive to Mantua, New Jersey.

. . .

When they finally arrived, Carlton came out and her dad seemed genuinely pleased to see his son-in-law. They shook hands warmly and then Carlton unloaded his suitcases from the car and took them inside.

For a moment her dad gazed around at the property. He was speechless. Her mom, talkative in her excitement, was telling him of how nice the place was and that there was even a swimming pool at the back.

"A swimming pool? Really?"

"Look, at the back there! —You can't see it?"

"Mom," Shaun said, "Dad will see everything in time. Come inside Dad..."

She welcomed him into her new home.

He thanked her and entered... looking around. "Bless the house," he said. "You do good, my daughter," he said, and opened his arms to her.

She hugged her Dad. This was a man she loved though they had not been close. For years back in Guyana their relationship could have been described as 'love-hate.' However, she had grown into regarding the past as the past and had forgiven him for all former indiscretions especially as it related to the way he once treated her mom. For now she only wanted their relationship to be redemptive. "Dad," she said at last. "I'm so glad to have you with us..."

"I'm glad too," she heard him say.

Then Carlton's mom hailed out, "Battery, boy! You back in America, boy!"

"Who's that?" he dad asked.

"That's Carlton's mother's voice, Dad..." Shaun said.

"How you doing, Miss Joyce?"

"Well I not feeling too good, but we going talk later, right?"

"Shaun, your father looking very tired..." her mom said

Shaun agreed. She wished him a good night's rest, and allowed her mom to take him away to her room.

Before Shaun headed off to her bed she stopped in to see her mother-in-law. "How you doing, Aunt Joyce?" she asked.

"So, so," Carlton's mom replied.

"You'll be okay, soon, Mom..."

"Meaning that you still taking me to the hospital in the morning..."

Shaun chuckled and echoed, "Still taking you to the hospital..."

. . .

She really didn't want to go but I knew something was wrong. It was a very interesting time for me. Back home it might have been said, 'When it rains, it pours,' or 'Old house on old house,' —both sayings having the same meaning more or less.

A few days earlier I had to take my mom to see a doctor for a minor surgery after they had found a lump in her breast for which a biopsy had been recommended in order to rule out Cancer. At that time my mother-in-law's stomach was paining her and compounded with that, her saliva had a reddish color. Somehow it didn't sit well with me, and since I was taking my mom to see a doctor, I thought it wise that Carlton's mom came along for a check up herself. She refused. (As far as mom was concerned, she had the minor surgery and the pathology came back negative for cancer and everyone concerned was grateful.)

After an exhausting day, I hugged Carlton, told him we needed to be up early the next day to take his Mom to the hospital, and I soon fell asleep.

Father's day broke with Carlton and I in bed, speaking about his mom's condition when the morning's quiet was shattered with my Mom screaming —running up the stairs.

"Carlton! —Oh God, Carlton!" She was pounding frantically at the bedroom door. "Your mother unconscious! —"Come quick! —"Help!"

I sprang out of bed thinking 911, grabbed the phone from the nightstand and made the call. Carlton rushed down the stair to his mother. His distraught sister was with her. I got dressed in record time and was soon with my mother-in-law as everyone stood around.

"What's wrong with her?" my dad asked, Carlton.

"I hope nothing serious," he stammered.

Joyce was indeed out, but she was breathing. I saw that she had vomited blood. I felt her pulse; it was weak, and just then the paramedics arrived.

They quickly hooked her up on their emergency life-support

system while I told them what medication she was on. They placed her on oxygen and prepped her for the emergency room. As they lifted her to the stretcher she came to, and weakly look at us. She looked confused.

"You're going to be alright, Aunt Joyce," I said as I squeezed her hand. "We're taking you to the hospital..."

Gloria, her daughter was visibly shaken, so was my Mom and Carlton, so someone had to be in control.

"Where would you like us to take her, please?" the Chief paramedic asked.

Immediately I had flashbacks of experiences with my dad during his sickness two years ago. I was not going to make the same mistakes.

"I would like her taken to Cooper Hospital, please," I said.

I turned to my father. "You're going to come with us, Dad?"

"No... I'm going to stay and watch the house..." he said and then gave me a hug of assurance. "Once you in charge, Shaun, everything's going to be okay... I *know* that!"

The ambulance took off with Joyce accompanied by her son. Gloria and my mother followed in my car, and soon we were at the Cooper Hospital's Emergency Room where they began to work on Carlton's mom right away.

They were able to stabilize her, but it had not been easy. Initially they attempted to check her stomach by introducing as a camera probe through her nostrils and into her stomach, but it was too much for Joyce who put up such a fight. They thought against it.

"I'm sorry," I said to the doctor. "This is the first time my Mother-in-law is in a hospital, so certain procedures will scare her..."

To the doctor it was incredulous. He, however, decided to have a battery of tests run on her. There was nothing else for us to do at the Emergency Room, so we told her that we were going to be back with her later that Sunday, and left a little after lunch. We had been at the hospital for over six hours.

We all got into my car and started home in mostly thoughtful silence until I said, "Imagine... the plan was for us to take her to the hospital... but instead God had it that she took ill this morning, and an ambulance had to rush her to the emergency room..." No one said anything. I guess they didn't know where I was going with what I was saying. "What I'm saying is this, if we had taken her ourselves, we might have still been at the emergency room waiting for them to look at her...

"Because the ambulance took her, however..."

"She's getting first class treatment," Carlton patched in.

My mother agreed.

Gloria was staring out the window that she had wound down. There were tears in her eyes, and I didn't know if it was because of her mother or because of the slipstreaming wind.

"Anyway," I said. "Aunt Joyce will be okay... all we need to do is to be positive... and pray she's in the right place for the help she needs..."

Gloria was crying.

Carlton turned to his sister. "Mommy's going to be alright," he said gently.

"This morning when I looked at mommy... I thought..." she began.

"I know what you thought," her brother said, "but mommy's going to be here a long time..."

"This morning... at that moment when I thought she was going to die... I realized how much I love my mother..."

"Aunt Joyce will be okay, Gloria," I said.

My mom agreed, and we drove the rest of the way in silence.

. . .

She spent three days in the Intense Care Unit. She needed Plasma; her blood pressure was unstable, and she also had gone through surgery to repair the ulcer.

I used to be there three times a day: early at mornings before I reported in to work, during my lunchtime, and at evenings after work. I was there every day for the duration of her stay. A few afternoons Carlton was able to visit her, but Gloria did not see her until that weekend.

She left the hospital seven days after being admitted, with prescriptions for medication and a list of restrictions to her diet.

During my mother-in-law's stay at the hospital, they had done a number of things to make her better. They did a cat scan of her heart, and it revealed a widening of her aorta. They even did a colonoscopy and removed a few polyps from her colon. As for the ulcers in her stomach, they discovered the pylori virus that caused them. She was lucky that the pathology showed negative for cancer. Aunt Joyce was given a new lease in life.

She had to make a follow-up visit to Dr. O who subsequently became our family doctor. He had seen my Dad, my Mom, my Husband, and now my mother-in-law.

On the day of the follow up visit, he saw my mother-in-law, and thought that once she rested and took her medication she was good as new. He was concerned more about me, however. "Having to take care of this amount of illness in your family, cannot be good for you, Shaun," he said. "How are you handing all of this?"

I said to him, "One day at a time doctor, one day at a time... It is my belief that God will not give me more than I can bear..."

CHAPTER 43: 2005
The Mantua Story Continues

REQUIEM FOR MY FATHER

My Dad had received his welcome letter and green card in less than a week. I was happy for him and Mom. But it was clear that he was not prepared to live for his wife and family, and things between us began to look shaky.

In my heart, my mom was my responsibility —not my dad's! He had disappointed her enough; he had hurt her enough, and I was not going to stand aside and see him hurt my mom the way she had been hurt countless times before by a man whose philandering ways seemed a feather in his cap. I had made a vow to take care of my Mom and not allow her to fall back into the life she had left four years ago back in Guyana. She had grown into being an independent woman. She had a good job, a bank account, and was taking care of herself.

My Dad it seemed found it very difficult to accept her that way, and sought to control her the way he did back in Guyana. It seemed that he was bent on returning to his old ways, and it seemed it was affecting his health. I saw signs that told me he was in danger of relapsing into his sickness of two years ago when we were in Maple Shade. I offered to take him to see Dr. O, but he refused to go; he said that he was okay.

Soon after, he left my home and went to stay with his sister—my aunt Desiree—in East Orange, a community with many Guyanese and other Caribbean nationals —a City where there was 'action,' where the lights were brighter and where he could have found many old friends.

Having left Mantua, however, things did not improve for my dad. He could not find a job in his field and was not willing to do anything else. Bit by bit he grew more agitated —more frustrated and began regretting he had left his country where a man could have been a man.

The year raced on. My in-laws' six-month stay was up. Aunt Joyce and her daughter had already returned to Guyana. Soon it was going to be Thanksgiving... soon it was going to be Christmas, and our families had planned that we'd all be at my home in Mantua for Thanksgiving, and at my Aunt Desiree's home for Christmas. Everyone, it seemed, were looking forward to the holidays here in America, everyone except my dad. He was there for both celebrations, however reluctantly and complaining about how cold and uncomfortable he was.

The new year broke and he began planning his return to Guyana. I wished he would not return, but no one, it seemed could have stopped him. So in the month of May he left for the airport without telling me that he was leaving... never really saying goodbye. He flew back to Guyana a sick man, and when he got back home he never called to tell me that he had arrived back safely.

It hurt.

Over the six months my dad's health deteriorated and then one night I had a dream about him lying in a bed and he was vomiting blood. It was as if I was in a room with him and yet invisible to him, and everywhere and everything in the room was covered in blood... and it was all emanating from his mouth.

That morning I awoke very distraught.

Three days later while at my desk at Blue Cross, the phone rang. It was around 9: A.M. and it was my aunt Desiree.

"Hello, Aunt Desiree..." She didn't respond immediately. Instead I heard her sigh on the line, and her husband murmuring low in the background.

My heart sank. It was like a knowing thing. Right away I knew it concerned the dream I had.

At last my aunt Desiree found her voice. "Shaun..."

"Yes, Aunt Desiree?"

"I hope you're sitting..."

My breath came fast and a creepy-crawly sensation enveloped my head. "Is it, Dad, Aunt Desiree? Is it Dad?"

"Yes..." she said. "We lost your Dad this morning... We just got the word..."

I was quiet for a while as I wrapped my thoughts around the news. And then I broke down as she talked and tried to comfort me.

. . .

SHAUN: Afterwards I was angry and hurt. In my mind my Dad had no reason to die. After all I had done to get him here as a U.S. resident —after all of the challenges I had to face to have gotten him here in America. Before he went back I had offered to take him to see the family doctor...

BASCOM: I guess you were hurt and bitter...

SHAUN: Bitter, yes! After all I had done for my father... (*Shakes her head.*) It was as if he did what he did to get back at me... After all I did for him... When he went back to Guyana was like spitting in my face for all I had done for him... He never thought of anyone but himself!

BASCOM: And I guess the fact that he had left without saying anything to you made it worse.

SHAUN: He had never said goodbye to me... so that day at my desk, I cried from more hurt than sadness of his death. (*Makes an open-palmed gesture of hopelessness.*) Then I was blaming myself for his death...

BASCOM: How so?

SHAUN: When he got back to Guyana, he didn't even call me. —Maybe *I* should have called and begged him to come back for me to take care of his health — maybe I should have gone home and insisted that he return with me...

BASCOM: No! I cannot agree there with you. Your father was a man! —His own man! He made a decision... he made a decision— (*Shrugs.*) What could you have done? Don't blame yourself.

SHAUN: (*Sighs.*) Well... he was dead. This news came when I was just about to re-launch my Pre-Paid Legal Services business... everything was set for me to get back into it...

BASCOM: But then you had to return home for your father's funeral...

SHAUN: Yes... At first I said that I was not going to go home for his funeral...

BASCOM: You were that angry.

SHAUN: I don't know what it was, but I started out not wanting to go home. But then I knew I just couldn't allow my mother to go home alone —to handle my dad's affairs and funeral all by herself... Thankfully, my dad's brother—my Uncle Gervy—managed to hold things together until me and my mom arrived... (*Shakes her head.*) It was a good thing I went home with her!

BASCOM: You realized that she would need you.

SHAUN: (*Nods and continues.*) She wouldn't have been able to handle it alone. There were lots of family rifts —there was a lot of strife going on, and I needed to be there to help arrange and handle things.

BASCOM: And your renewed thrust into your PPLSI business? I guess that had to take another backseat again?

SHAUN: (*Shakes her head.*) I refused to give up on my PPLSI business. I dried my tears, straightened my back, and prepared to push forward. Somehow my Dad's death opened my eyes to the world in a whole new way —his death made me realize how fragile and unpredictable life was... and that we have to do all we could each day we're given, to make it count, and make a difference...

BASCOM: I guess your business was put on just a brief hold until you returned from the wedding—

SHAUN: Funeral—

BASCOM: I'm sorry —funeral...

SHAUN: We booked our flight. Carlton traveled home with me and my Mom.

BASCOM: I guess a lot of other relatives —his sisters —brothers flew in for the funeral too...

SHAUN: My aunt Desiree, uncle David and his wife traveled home for the funeral...

BASCOM: You said that you went with your mother primarily because there were rifts in the family... you actually said there was 'strife' that was going on. Can you talk a bit about that?

SHAUN: No... (*Shakes her head.*) I rather let that be. It doesn't have to be in the book. Suffice to say, however... (*Shakes her head.*) that I have forgiven my stepbrother for the things that he did. But if I hadn't flown home with my mom, she would not have gotten anything much from her husband's estate.

BASCOM: Thanks to your intervention...

SHAUN: When we were children, my mom took care of my two stepbrothers as though they too were her children? (*Sighs.*) I never knew we had different mothers until I was about 9 or 10 years old.

· · ·

It was difficult with all the family contention. Had I not been there my mom would not have made it through. I had only been given a three-day leave of compassion from my Blue Cross job and had to travel back the day after the funeral. My brother was left to protect my mom for the rest of the week after the burial.

On the flight home, I thought of the funeral. I had looked at my dad in his casket. He no longer suffered as I heard he had, in his last days. I looked into my Dad's face, so emaciated in death, and said my goodbye to him. "No hard feelings, dad," I whispered. "I have forgiven you... and I hope you have forgiven me... all is forgiven..."

CHAPTER 44: 2006
The Mantua Story Continues

RETURN TO IN-VITRO.

January 2006. Much had changed. All the in-laws were gone, and my mom only came home on weekends. We were now alone in our new home, and alone Carlton and I reflected on the year past. On the home front we had accomplished much. Now we faced the new year with decisions of moving forward.

One night in January, Carlton said to me, "This is 2006, Babes... What are we going to do about a baby? Do you remember you said you'd put it off until this year?"

"Do you think it ever leaves my mind, Carlton?" I shook my head. "Every time I see a baby's carriage I think about it... about if the In-Vitro thing is going to work..."

"Babes," he said. "You have to think that it's going to work!"

"When the winter breaks we'll arrange to see Dr. C on the follow-up steps we have to take... Maybe around June... —July..."

Soon after, I scheduled our annual check up with Dr. O. All lab work on me came back normal, so we thought the time was right for us to try In-vitro fertilization. Come June, we were going to do it.

. . .

At last the time came. I made an appointment, and we met with Dr. C. He was happy we had made the decision to try for our fist baby through IVF, and soon after, his team to began preparing us for the In-vitro fertilization process. We had a nurse assigned to us specifically and she wrote prescriptions for all the fertility medication I would have needed for the duration of the treatment.

Part of the IVF process involved me administering a special

injection to myself. She painstakingly showed me and Carlton how it was to be done. The correct dosage that had to be drawn into the needle for me to inject myself was of absolute importance.

I said, "It's the self-injecting part that worries me..." Then I turned to Carlton. "It might work out better if you do it for me, you know..."

But he was hesitant about it. "I don't know..." he said.

"It's easy," the nurse said. "Anyone of you would be able to do it. You'll do okay, Mr. Stephenson."

We were given a kit with medication and different sizes of needles that were to be used in a thirty-day process. It was explained that self-injecting was going to effectively stop my period —which was a prerequisite for the In-Vitro fertilization. The process had to begin from the very last day of my period and continue at nights and mornings for twenty-eight days. I had to be first injected in my belly, and later in my thighs, and lastly in my butt. The prospect of being a human pincushion for almost a month was daunting. But that I stood to make a baby for my husband after it all, would erase every form of discomfiture I would have gone through.

We did what had to be done in preparation and I was ready to proceed with the In-Vitro. All was set. I cut back some of my hours of work in order to relax and not be too tired during the process. I had daily lab work and ultra –sounds. As the medication began to act I was producing dozens of follicles that were maturing so quickly, they had to adjust my medication. Coming down to the last two weeks, the effects on my body startled me. I grew very bloated and my pelvic area started to feel so heavy. They told me that there were over twenty follicles in each of my ovaries and Dr. C was pleased. The entire office was amazed at my progress. They explained to Carlton and me that it was normally difficult for the average patient, going through In-vitro, to produce a single egg.

The day was drawing near for retrieval and on that last stretch of twenty-four hours before the retrieval began, I was scheduled to inject myself with a prescribed medication, and of a dosage that had to be precise —exact. There was no room for a mistake.

So that night I drew the medication into the large needle and carefully injected myself. As I withdrew the needle I realized that I had done something wrong. I grabbed for the notes I had been given... read into it and sighed despondently. I did not give myself the correct dosage, and I could not undo the mistake.

I called the nurse early the next morning and told her what I had done. She informed Dr. C. He, in turn, called, and listened to me. Afterwards he told me it was okay and that, nevertheless, they were going to move forward with retrieval as planned, and that Carlton had to be there to give sperm.

Deep down I felt devastated; I had screwed up with the dosage and didn't have much hope. But since the doctor himself told me that what I thought I had done was apparently no big thing, I began thinking that maybe I did do it right —that maybe the mistake was all in my mind.

The retrieval was supposed to be a simple procedure, but I had to be put under, however.

"Are you ready, Shaun?" Dr. C said.

"Yes, doctor... I am..."

"Everything's going to be well..." he said.

And I fell into sweet nothingness.

When I opened my eyes, seemingly a second later, Carlton was there watching over me. He touched my face.

"Good to have you back, Babes," he said.

I smiled feeling a little woozy.

Dr. C came over and he looked pleased.

"We have a total of twenty-three eggs," he said smiling. "What we'll do is use all of them and pick the best two or three for insemination, once all goes well in four days time..."

"So far so good, doctor?" Carlton said.

"So far, so good," echoed Dr. C. "The sperm specimens are healthy. All seem to be on target, Mr. Stephenson."

"My wife and I are going to pray..."

"Nothing beats prayer... so we'll see you and Shaun in four or five days. You'll get a call from us..."

. . .

Carlton drove us home. I was glad to be over for now. I just needed to just get into bed. One month of anticipation and the strange medication had taken a toll on my body and my emotions.

On the first day after the retrieval, Dr. C called me daily to inform me all was well and thing were looking good according to schedule he even commented on the condition of the eggs said they were by far the best they had to work with compared to others. I told Carlton the details and he was pleased too. On the second and third day, he called and the optimism was high.

On the fourth day, however, the phone rang and it was Dr. C. "Hi, Dr. C," I answered excitedly.

"Hello, Shaun," he said, and there was no optimism in his voice. I felt it.

"Is everything, okay, doctor?"

"Is your husband around, Shaun?"

"He's at work, Doctor... What is it, Doctor?"

He began by saying he had never seen anything like it, then continued, "Mrs. Shaun... I had all the confidence that things were going to be okay, but..."

"What happened, Doctor?" My voice shook and I felt hollow inside.

"The eggs... have begun disintegrating, Mrs. Stephenson. I cannot follow through with the insemination. None of the eggs got to the stage of blastocyst..."

"I understand, Doctor..." I could have said nothing more. Deep down I knew, I knew, I knew, I knew, I knew that it was not going to work out.

"Mrs. Stephenson?"

"Thank you for all your help, Doctor..." I couldn't hold back my tears. Oh God! I felt awful! "Thank you, Dr. C..."

"I'm sorry," he said. "But you do know that this process is covered by your Health Insurance, and that you do have three more attempts at it..."

"I know, Doctor... I'll stay in touch, Doctor..."

I hung up.

. . .

I wanted to put this ordeal behind me for a long time. I had made up my mind: I was not going to attempt In-Vitro again anytime soon. Any hope of a child would have to be a miracle because I only had one tube. Carlton too was devastated but tried to comfort me. "Let's talk about it, Babes," he said that night. I told him no, that I had gone through enough!

"Carlton," I said, weeping. "All I want to do now, is put the whole thing behind me..."

He hugged me.

I guess I had to learn to live fending off the question: When do you plan on having children, Shaun? And I guess I had to learn to live with the reality that I might never have a child of my own.

CHAPTER 45: 2006
The Mantua Story Continues

TRANSCENDENTAL MELTDOWN AND REVELATION

September 2006. Las Vegas. Shaun Stephenson came for the Pre-Paid Legal Services Convention with the expectation that she would be staying in a modest room at the MGM Grand Hotel. She was, however, pleasantly surprised about the promotional bonus that upgraded her to a luxury suite.

She entered a huge furnished room and was immediately drawn to the vast picture window with the heavy drapes mammoth king-sized bed with an architectural wonder of a headboard carrying a check pattern made from two hues of brown wooden panels. A pair of in by nightstands like chests with a huge lamp on each hemmed the great bed in. The spread that covered it was of a thick and heavy material that looked like some sort of tapestry.

Just inside the vast window—offering a view to Tropicana and Las Vegas Boulevard where the great, gilded, MGM lion rose majestically above the intersection—was a stylish leather couch fit for a roman emperor. Next to it was a large oval shaped coffee table. Over from the great bed was a comfortable seating arrangement with a large TV set over from yet another coffee table.

There was also a kitchenette. She sought out the shower, opened a door, and found herself in a large, glitzy bathroom with that even had a Jacuzzi.

The effects of the suite, however, did not last on her. As vast as it was, so was the anguish that was bearing down on her.

Shaun Stephenson sat on the edge of the huge bed and was truly alone with her God, as she looked deep within herself for answers. She thought of her father and how he left without saying goodbye; she thought of her seven miscarriages, she thought of the failed In-Vitro fertilization... She thought of Carlton... and her tears began to flow even though she made not a sound. The river of pain within her had crested its banks. A levy deep within her resolve was cracking. There has been so much, so much, so much pain... there had been so much pain and disappointment in her life. She shook her head. "Why?" she whispered as her tears coursed down and between her fingers encasing her face. "What is it that I have done wrong? ...Oh, God! ...What is it that I am *doing* wrong?"

She thought of Carlton. She had wanted him to be with her. "What's the point in me coming?" he asked her. "What am I going to do while you're at your Convention with your Pre-Paid Legal Associates? ... I already know how it feels to be disregarded, disrespected, and ignored, Shaun! You never have time for me here in New Jersey! What? You want me to know how it feels to be disregarded, disrespected, and ignored in Las Vegas? I'm sorry, Babes... but I rather not stand in your way..."

She sat huddled on the edge of a great bed in a luxurious MGM Grand suite and began sobbing in her palms... and soon she was on her knees on the thickly carpeted floor...

. . .

On that evening of September 11th, 2006, my life hung in a balance. I prayed and cried to God for help. I was alone on a search for my purpose in life. I had gone through so much with family... I had hit rock bottom emotionally, spiritually and financially. My Pre-Paid Legal Services business was pushed back, and *I* was pushed back taking care of everyone else. I kneeled in that hotel room in desperate need of help, and I cried to the only source I knew since a child. God! God never leaves! I told myself, "God never leaves!" He did not bring me this far to leave me. For how many hours I was on my knees I cannot recall, but I was a long time on my knees —pleading —begging God for direction — *Who am I? —Why am I here? —What is my purpose here, Lord?*

The next morning I awoke, feeling slightly drained, and thanked God for a new day. But in my mind was the word 'Gideon.' I lay staring at the ceiling for a while trying to figure what it meant. I reached over to the nightstand, grabbed my handbag in which I kept my pocket bible, but discovered that I did not pack it. *Hotel rooms always carry bibles,* I thought and sat up. I pulled open the drawer of the nightstand on my right, found a Bible, and printed on the Cover were the words: 'Placed by the Gideons.'

An eerie feeling enveloped me. Back in my country, Guyana, one might say, "My head grew."

Looking for answers, I began to page through the Bible, came upon the Header, 'Who are the Gideons?' and I began to read. The account was fascinating. It was the story of three traveling strangers who came together and named themselves after Gideon, a biblical prophet of Israel, through whom God was able to do much for his people. This was a band of believers whom had dedicated their lives to the service of God.

I read the biblical story but I still needed answers. For some reason, Chapter 16 of the book of Mark came to mind. It was an account of Christ having been risen from the dead. The message he gave was to spread the word to every creature... and things began to slowly make sense. Deep down I guessed I was seeking some form of spiritual confirmation that PPLSI was the right vehicle for me to fulfill my purpose of being a voice for those who didn't have one, and living a life of Service to Mankind.

I had told myself that it was God who led me to be in Las Vegas that September... —I thought as much. After I listened to the 'dare-to-dream' speech given by Mr. Harland Stonecipher, everything crystallized for me, and I knew that I had found the answers I sought.

"Where there is no vision, the people perish..." he had said, quoting from Proverbs Chapter 29.

"There is no mysterious hand or force out there to stop you. The only force that will stop you is you... Your success or failure at Pre-Paid Legal is totally in your control as you leave here tonight...

"My vision for Pre-paid Legal and for each of you has never been more clear nor have I ever been more dedicated. I want to share my vision with you... I want to help you dream your dreams and help you make your dreams come true... I want to help you find your calling. I want you to dare to dream that things can be better for you tomorrow than today no matter how great or bad today is...

"I am daring you tonight to make a decision, a commitment to change your life and make a living while making a difference in people's lives. I challenge you to do well by doing good. Answer your calling! Do what you were put here to do. Help other people..."

When I was leaving Las Vegas the last bit of Mr. Stonecipher's speech echoed in my mind... *Because dreams can, and do come true when you discover your true calling*...and in my mind, nothing was going to stop me.

I left Vegas knowing that I could not continue on the path I was: working day-in day-out for a paycheck —building the future for a group of executives —and securing someone else's future. Some of my associates called me Mrs. Blue Cross and of late it wasn't a moniker to be proud about. I had to make changes in my life if I was to achieve anything that I had prayed and asked direction for. I knew that there was no way I was going to make a difference in peoples lives unless I worked hard to achieve it.

I was now determined to ignite my PPLSI business and so set about putting a plan in place to resuscitate business relationships that I had built over the years. Prior to leaving Vegas I spoke with Pre-Paid legal Executive Director David Allen, requested his help in jump-starting my business the following month, and, again, he agreed to help me.

. . .

Things were still up in the air after my return from Vegas and the Death of my Dad, but I went ahead with plans for the re-launch of my business. It was a difficult choice.

While being a guest at my home, David Allen was scheduled to attend a series of events beginning with a Private business reception at my home. It was a success. Several of my associates, friends, and relatives were there to join Carlton my mom in the modest celebration in our Mantua home.

My jovial friend Bruce Hayes catered my business re-launch. He prepared an array of excellent dishes artistically displayed. There was an ice carving onto which the slogan, *Equal Access, Justice for all*, was carved. There was also a fountain with punch.

Many commented that the occasion felt like a wedding reception. Bruce out-did himself.

By the time the evening was over, we signed up several memberships and over five associates.

That night I lay in bed feeling grateful about how things had gone. I felt Carlton's eyes upon me. "What?" I said.

"You're smiling to yourself, Babes," he said.

"Isn't that good?"

"That's good," he said. "So, what next? —the church presentation you told me about?"

"Yes... I have to meet with Pastor Evans..."

CHAPTER 46: 2006
The Mantua Story Continues

MEETING REV. TONY C. EVANS, SR.

After I had returned from Las Vegas that September, I planned on calling on Reverend Tony Evans. I prayed that he would help me in my business endeavor as a PPLSI Independent Associate. I telephoned him, and he had agreed to meet with me. I met him at his City Office, and he said to me, "Shaun... it has been a while..."

. . .

BASCOM: Him saying that it had been a while, infers that the two of you met before. Tell me about 'meeting Rev. Evans.'

SHAUN: Okay... Back in 2003, I had started to attend lots of networking and other chamber events as I continued to build my PPLSI business. At that time Mr. Ken Evans, membership representative of the State Chamber, was trying to help by referring me to business owners and other individuals who he felt would be good contacts for my business. Two of those individuals are now very good friends of mine that have come to know my family...

BASCOM: One was Rev. Evans...

SHAUN: And the other was Mr. Jonah Cooper —but you're asking about Rev. Evans, so let me give you details on meeting him. Ken Evans called one day and said he had a good contact for me, and gave me Rev Evans' number. He was an assistant to the Mayor of

Camden at the time we met. He is now the Director of Health and Human Service for the City of Camden. Anyway, I called his office, got his voice mail and left him a message indicating Mr. Ken Evans felt I needed to meet with him.

BASCOM: And you left your phone number...

SHAUN: He calls me back that very day and asked how he may be of assistance. (*Shrugs.*) I requested a short meeting with him so that I might share some information that might be mutually beneficial to each other. He told me that twelve-noon the following day worked for him. It worked for me also... (*Shrugs.*) I called Ken Evans and thanked him for putting me in touch...

. . .

Shaun Stephenson sat with Rev. Tony C. Evans one week before she was scheduled to re-launch her business as a catered event at her Mantua home. As he spoke to someone on the phone, her mind went back to the very first time she had met him.

She had prepared a folder with brochures and applications and other news pieces for talking points, for their meeting.

She got to Camden's City Hall with time to spare, so sat in her car until it was time, and with the directions he had given her, found his office quite easily. She rapped on the already opened door.

Rev. Evans, a man who seemed to be wrapped in a smile, welcomed her in.

"How are you today, Mrs. Stephenson?" he had said.

"Blessed and grateful to you for taking a few minutes of your time to see me," she said, elegant in her dark business suit. "And if you don't mind, you can call me, Shaun..."

"I don't mind at all," he said jovially and invited her to sit —to make herself comfortable. "My job," he continued, "is helping people... and being a Pastor I am even more dedicated to helping folks on their walk of Faith. So, Shaun, tell me about yourself and what I can do to help you..."

She, instead, began by asking him how long he had been with the city, and what were his responsibilities as an assistant to the Mayor. She thought it was important getting to know about him before she got into speaking to him about Pre-Paid Legal Services Incorporated and her being a PPLSI Independent Associate.

He didn't hesitate to speak, and so she learned about his amazing career —about him being born and educated in Chicago, and how he came to now be in New Jersey.

She then launched into telling him about Pre-Paid legal. Among the things she shared with him were her goals. "I would like to educate people on why they need to have a legal plan in place..."

"I am already familiar with your company, Shaun," he said. "Other individuals have approached me about this. Now, if you're asking yourself, 'Why did he allow me to explain something he knew about all the time?' I'll say this to you: No one really took the time to explain these services the way you did..."

"Thank you, Reverend Evans..."

"I thank *you*, Shaun. So tell me how you think I can help you..."

"Well, Reverend Evans, I was hoping that with your assistance I might be able to do presentations for Churches and other organizations you may be affiliated with..."

He smiled and reached for his telephone. He called up a friend who was also a Pastor to be part of the discussion. "Pastor Martinez," Rev. Evans said as he hung up the phone, "has an office just down the hall. What we're going to do is, put our heads together to see how we can help your business along..."

"Thank you..."

And so it was that she met Pastor Martinez and he was also very interested.

In the end, Rev. Evans promised her that he would review all the documents Shaun Stephenson left and that she should follow up with him in a few days. It had been a very promising meeting. Shaun felt that she had indeed accomplished something very significant. In her mind she felt it had been the beginning of a very fruitful relationship.

Just weeks later, however, her Dad arrived from Guyana to stay with her. It turned out that he was very ill, and she had to take care of him. Being she was so caught up with her father's medical care the follow-up call Rev. Evans anticipated from her was not made. She called him later, however —apologized for not getting back to him sooner, and asked that he give her a few weeks to take care of family issues.

He was very understanding...

But 'a few weeks' turned into months and then into years through which she did call him occasionally to see how he had been doing, and he would invite her to the 10th Street, Baptist Church where he was Pastor in Camden.

. . .

He hung up the telephone. It was October 2006. She was sitting once again with Reverend Tony Evans, who man whose life still felt as though it was wrapped in a smile.

"Where were we, Shaun?" he said.

"You were inviting me to see your church and the space we'd be able to use for the presentation, come Sunday..." I said.

"Oh yes... that's where we were. "

"So Wednesday night it is."

"Wednesday night it is —God willing..."

. . .

There was a rainstorm that Wednesday night, but I showed up anyway. As I entered the church, there were a few ladies in the lobby area and a gentleman who welcomed me so warmly. "Can I help you, my dear?" he said.

I told them that Reverend Evans had invited me to come see the church and that he would be there to show me around. The gentleman made a call, reached Reverend Evans, and hung up and said to me with a smile, "He's on his way. Why don't you make yourself comfortable in the meantime?"

"Thank you..." I was surprised that, despite the inclement weather he was going to be there.

I later learned that the ladies I had met were the Pastor's aides that he called his 'Golden Girls': Sister Dorothy, Sister Lucille, and

Sister Chris. I learned too that the kind gentleman who greeted me was Carl, one of the associate ministers at the Church.

Rev. Evans arrived all bright and enthused as though he had just walked in from a sunny and beautiful day. He broke into a smile when he saw me. "So you did not allow the weather to stop you," he said.

"I was hoping that the storm did not stop *you*, reverend Evans," I said, and Carl laughed.

"Oh no!" Reverend Evans retorted, laughing. "I'll go through any storm to do God's work…"

One of the women said, "Amen…"

That night he was having a bible-teaching session and I sat in. His commitment and sincerity was unmistakable. Afterwards he took me on a tour of the entire building.

That Sunday, he welcomed David Allen and I with open arms. We sat through the service. I discovered that Reverend was a great teacher of The Word. At the end of it, he announced from the pulpit that David and I were there to share valuable and important information on Identity Theft and Legal Services down in the Fellowship Hall in the basement for all interested.

Reverend Evans along with several of his members attended. After David Allen had done the presentation, Rev. Evans set the example by signing up for the Service, and others followed his lead and signed up. It was a good time of sharing and learning.

Meeting Pastor Tony C. Evans, Sr. was indeed a blessing.

After the presentation, he reminded me about the very first time we met back in 2003. "Back then," he said to me. "I told you back then that God had a plan for your life, remember?"

I remembered not responding verbally but it made me think… *here we are today almost three years later, and I'm here in his Church after a Pre-Paid legal Services presentation…*

· · ·

Our relationship began to bloom and he invited me to come and have fellowship anytime. The warmth I felt on that very first visit that stormy night continued, and somehow I knew there must be a reason why Rev came into my life.

He began to share his life story with me. Through our many

conversations I learned, that as part of his career, he had been in upper management positions with major consumer-product corporations, and the top executive for his own entertainment-marketing firm. This revelation was encouraging. His knowledge of business was extensive and fascinating and I got lot of tips from him.

He also became my spiritual father and mentor, and for a while I felt torn between the Living Faith mega church and what I sensed was my newfound spiritual home at 10ᵗʰ Street, Baptist. In my three years of attending the mega church I had never met the Pastor one-on-one. And here I was at 10ᵗʰ Street Baptist feeling at home —feeling welcome, and in my heart I knew I could be of service here.

It seemed Rev Evans read my mind: "So Shaun," he said to me. "When are you going to join us? —I shall continue to pray for you being with us soon."

I smiled. "If it be God's will, I'll be obedient," I said.

A few months following my mom and I attended a Sunday Service at 10ᵗʰ Street Baptist. When the altar call was made to accept Christ, and come by way of candidate for Baptism, Christian experience, and membership, I sat frozen in my seat —torn between whether I should join or continue to attend the Living Faith mega Church? Then as Rev made the final call for anyone else, a feeling of peace came over me, I got to my feet, went to the alter, and accepted the invitation to be a member of 10ᵗʰ Street Baptist Church.

I met the entire congregation and was overjoyed. Everyone welcomed me. I attended a class for new members called 'discipleship.' Rev. Evans was our teacher, and did a great job at breaking down the details of the Bible along with the 'Articles Of Faith.' His teachings on the interpretation and application of God's Word were both, inspiring and very practical. It was fulfilling to be part of his congregation.

Rev Evans had an open door policy, which meant that I could have asked his support and advice on any matter. I chose to seek his assistance in building my Pre-Paid Legal Service business since his suggestions were always very good. When the City sponsored the Identity Theft Seminar for seniors, Rev. Evans and his staff did the outreach. They had invited over 150 seniors. He also did the opening remarks.

It turned out to be a great session and might not have been without him. He promised that he would assist, and helped me with my PPLSI business, and he kept his word.

CHAPTER 47: 2006 - 2007

The Mantua Story Continues

REQUIEM FOR MY GRANDPA

It was summer once more. Carlton and I went back to our lives without a child, and I was working longer hours once again. Carlton now worked overtime and also on Saturdays.

Lately my Grandpa kept coming to my mind. I had found out that he was then in living in Montclair, New Jersey with someone, whom we all believed, was taking good care of him. But somehow he kept coming to mind and I didn't know why. Maybe it had been because I was thinking of my dad... his son. I had called the apartment where my grandpa was supposed to be living and spoke with him. He was happy to hear from me, but he didn't sound too well, and I was troubled. I spoke with the person he lived with, and informed her that his relatives were going to drop by to see him that Christmas day.

The 25th of December came and a group of us started off for Montclair bearing gifts. It was myself, Carlton, LaToya and Deanna (two of grandpa's grandchildren), and my mom. When we got there, however, there was no one at home. It was a terrible disappointment.

It was not until early in 2006 that I was able to reach him by phone. After then I began calling daily to hear how he was, and he always told me that he was getting along okay. To me his voice said something else. Deep inside I felt that he was not okay as he continually claimed.

"Grandpa," I said to him. "Let me come get you so that you could spend some time with me, you know... —so you can see another place and be among family for a while... What you say?"

"Well... me grand child... that would be so nice..."

Mother's Day May 2006, I drove with my Mom to Montclair to pick up my Grandpa. As I entered the little room where he stayed and laid eyes on him my heart sank. I was saddened and concerned. He did not look at all well. He looked so wasted... so weak —like a man hanging on by his broken fingernails. He was his old talkative self, however. "Let's go, Grandpa," I said, and he rose shakily to his feet and started for the door as though he wanted to leave the little room in a hurry. Mom followed him, and helped him down the stair, while I gathered his things.

After I left the room, and saw that my mom was still walking with him to my vehicle, and I could have seen that he was moving with difficulty —as if walking was a task for him. When they got to the Ford Explorer, he leaned onto it. When I got to the vehicle, he was breathing very short.

"How you're feeling, Grandpa?"

"Alright," he gasped.

My mom put the two bags with his stuff in the back and climbed in.

"Sit down, Grandpa..." I said. "Let's go..."

He tried to pull himself up and into the front passenger seat, but he wasn't able, and his breathing was labored.

"Let me help you, Grandpa," I said and boosted him as best as I could, and he made it.

My mom and I exchanged concerned glances.

As we headed home he seemed exhausted and soon fell asleep. When we arrived in Mantua, I woke him, and we helped him into the house. He seemed glad to have finally reached my home.

When I got him inside he was happy to see Carlton. After I settled him in his room and told him to rest, I sat by his bedside and questioned him about how he was feeling, and what he was feeling exactly in his body, and I also asked him to show me what medication he was taking. He said that he had a swollen prostate. But I suspected that it might have been more than that and made the decision on the spot, to take him to see Dr. O.

I took a few days off from work, the doctor examined my grandpa, and recommended that I take him to see a Urologist, and I did. The Urologist examined him and said he had congestive heart failure and recommended, among other things, that we kept my grandpa's feet elevated. As a follow-up I took him the next day to the Cooper Hospital's Emergency Room. I told them as much as I knew about his condition and that he had been seeing a doctor in Montclair where he lived. (I let them know that he was only spending some time with me.)

They did a few X-rays, and told me that they were not going to keep him —that he needed to go back to his doctor in Montclair for a follow-up. This outrage me at first, but then I calmed down. In principle they were probably right since I told them he already had doctor.

I began to think, *What next?*

Cooper had, however, prescribed a stronger dose of the water pill he was already on, in order to reduce the build up of water in his body which was very troubling: Grandpa could not hold his urine and there were repeated 'accidents.' When he felt he wanted to 'pass water' it was often too late. Because his hands shook and could not help himself fast enough, I had to accompany him many times.

The new pills were causing him to pass water more frequently and I knew he would require constant assistance. This presented a challenge for me because I had to be at work. I could not have stayed at home all week to assist him, so there were lots of decisions to be made.

I decided on getting him 'Depends.' He didn't like them but gave in to putting them on. I remember that he shook his graying head and mumbled something to the effect of 'Once a man, twice a baby.' This used to be my strongest protector; I too was affected by seeing him in depends, but it was the best thing I could have thought of at that time to save him from the discomfiture of being wet. At nights I reverted to laying a sheet of plastic below his bedding and padding it with extra towels.

I also saw that he found it very difficult getting in and out of his bed because his feet were so tightly swollen, they felt like wood. I used to be at my Blue Cross job thinking about him home alone... praying that he would be okay when I got back. When I looked at his face and tummy I could have seen how much water was in him, and this only made it harder on his heart. He would take a few steps and would be breathless. So being at work and thinking about him was very troubling. He just couldn't have helped himself much. My grandfather definitely was in need of emergency care; and I definitely needed help taking care of him.

I had to call on our family. There was no way I could have done it alone, and I thought of his daughter... my aunt Desiree.

At that point there had been an old coldness between my grandpa and her. They hadn't spoken to each other for years. Each wanted nothing to do with the other. I called my aunt Desiree anyway, and her love for her father made the difference. She allowed bygones to be bygones and committed to helping her Dad. She asked me what exactly was wrong with him and I provided her some details on his sickness. "There might be other things affecting him that I don't know, Aunt Desiree," I said, "but what I do know is that we need to get him in *UMDNJ* right away!"

"Okay, Shaun," my aunt Desiree said. "Okay... I'm going to come up with your Mom on the train to Hamilton, so that I can get up by you; and tomorrow, Saturday, we're going to take him to *UMDNJ* Emergency Room, okay?"

"Thank you, Aunt Desiree..."

"That's what family for, girl Shaun. I have to thank you for looking out for him..."

. . .

Memories of my Dad's sickness... my mother-in-law's sickness flooded back, and I thought, *I am always running with family to emergency rooms*. And as I drove my grandfather to the University of Medicine and dentistry of New Jersey, I prayed that Grandpa got admitted. I guess that my aunt and my mom who were with were praying the same.

We got there in good time and signed him in. After he was wheeled to a bed, a nurse checked his pulse and blood pressure. She looked at the reading and showed it to me. It was so low it was a miracle that he was alive, and was admitted. Congestive Heart Failure was just one of other major medical issues that had to be addressed.

For the past ten years my grandpa had been having a very difficult life in America, but I never knew until, lying in bed one day, he began to confide in me. I listened and wept. I looked at him... what he had been reduced to, and wept.

This was the man who took care of me as a baby; I grew up

with him. This was a man who would have given the world for his grandchildren. My grandpa was a provider to all of his grandchildren... He made sure we were never in need —tried to give us everything we asked for. Every tree that he planted was for his grandchildren. The large garden massaged by the wind from the nearby river was a garden he labored over for his grandchildren.

To see him weak in bed broke my heart.

Hadn't I driven to Montclair and gotten him, he would have died soon after. The doctor explained how critical his condition was. They were amazed he did not have a heart attack. They promised, however, that they would have done the best they could for him, and they did.

Grandpa spent several days in the hospital, and when he was discharged he was like a baby. He could not walk or do anything for himself, but his daughter took him to her home in East Orange to take care of him.

LaToya, my aunt's eldest daughter, gave up her room for her grandfather, but she contributed much more. At that time, she was in College Studying to be a Registered Nurse, and it was because of her training at hospitals during her 'clinicals,' that she was able to clean him, turn him, and change his 'Pampers.' My grandfather, at that time, was close to skeletal. He was so thin his skin bruised easily, but with LaToya there for him, bruises due to his thinness, and bedsores due to him being laid up in bed, never developed. LaToya also made sure he got his right dosage of medication each day.

Deanna, LaToya's younger sister who was then in high school, helped to take care of her grandfather also. She looked forward to feeding him and helping in whatever ways she could. This was an old man who was special to her.

When she was a baby, her mother, finding it difficult to take care of her because of work and other pressing commitments in America, had sent Deanna back to Guyana to live a while with him and her grandmother Daphne. They became her parents until she was five years old and was returned to America where began Nursery school.

Deanna had become the apple of grandpa's eyes and it hurt her to see what his illness had done to him.

More than anything else the family had a chance to heal while caring and loving grandpa.

He needed general assistance at home, but because he had no Health insurance, Joe, my aunt's husband—who worked at more than one nursing home and knew a lot about geriatric care—helped to take care of my grandfather. He and my Uncle Joe became very close.

There was a lot of expensive medication that he needed, but we did the best we could. I visited him often and helped with his nutrition. In the end he began to recover slowly, but surely.

. . .

I visited him three to four times per week. I talked to him a lot. I knew how proud and independent he had always been, and would tell him things like, "Grandpa, you will walk again, and you will soon be going to the bathroom again by yourself... but until then, we will take care of you..."

The months went by and he got better. There were a few scares here and there, but he bounced back. Soon he began to walk again, was able to go to the bathroom by himself, and no longer needed adult pampers for insurance. We still had to feed him, though, because both of his hands shook so violently he found it hard to handle a spoon or a fork.

During his recuperation he reconnected with Christian, a friend he had made back in Montclair. Christian and his wife called him 'Uncle' and looked out for him when he lived in Montclair. After he got back on his feet, they visited him in East Orange as often as they could, and would pick him up on Sundays to take him to church.

My grandfather graced our lives for almost another year until he took ill once again on April of 2006. This time there wasn't much the doctors could have done for him, and he knew it. As a family, we all decided that my grandpa be allowed to make his peace at home with his daughter, his grandchildren, and his son-in-law and good friend, Joe. Grandpa died on May 31st 2007. He was eighty-two years old, and I loved him.

CHAPTER 48: 2007
The Mantua Story Continues

ECHOES FROM A GETHSEMANE STATE OF MIND

She stood outside the U.S. Embassy in Duke Street, Kingston in Georgetown, quietly awaiting her turn to be interviewed; and quietly awaiting her fate, she had prayed. Is today the first day of my destiny? She stood before the window where the Consular Officer waited with piercing blue eyes and a rather unusual physiological challenge presented itself: remembering how to breathe calmly. "What is your career plan? "What are you doing now—in terms of employment? "Do you plan to remain in banking? "What plans do you have for the future? "How long do you wish to stay in the United States? "When do you plan returning to Guyana? ..." She had been prepared and mixed truth and half-truths skillfully. In the end she convinced him that she was going to return and not destined to be yet another of the tens-of-thousands never to honor the granted temporary visa. She was asked to come back to the Embassy in order to pick up her passport that she had obtained some seven years before. She always believed that one day she was going to be able to travel to the United States...

The time was 4:30 A.M. and Shaun Stephenson was in tears and once again on her knees as she had been a few months ago in Las Vegas when that feeling of emptiness —of loss and loneliness had weighed heavily on her soul. She was praying for answers then, like she was fasting for answers now. Her journey, that began fourteen years ago, flashed through her mind. *My journey has been hard... my journey as been painful... How could I have come this far not knowing my destiny? Why am I on this road, Lord? What is my purpose? I know I've asked it before? Why has my journey been so hard?*

There were so many painful markers along the way and at the

beginning they were barbs that pierced her heart. She wept so long and so loud she lost her voice. The pain was so much.

Where is it all going to end? When will the pain stop?

What do I have to do to tear this anguish I feel so intensely from my heart?

"I need to know my mission in life, Lord? Make me your vessel, Lord!"

And her mom, gently massaging between her daughter's shoulder blades, crooned, "God willing, my child, God willing..."

One Sunday a televangelist did a sermon on fasting and Shaun remembered how difficult it had been to try so many years ago. She never could have done it for even half a day.

As she wept on her knees, and as her mom kept her company that wintry morning in January 2007, Shaun Stephenson had begun a twenty-one-day Daniel Fast during which no sweet, breads, meat or fish of any kind should be eaten. It was a fast that requires only the consumption of water, vegetables and fruit. Her mom decided to do it with her. They agreed to pray together each morning at 4: A.M. After Shaun's alarm went off, she would call her mom and for an hour or more they prayed for answers together.

While she was into the Daniel fast Shaun came across the biblical account of Moses spending forty days on Mt. Sinai, off which he came with the 10 commandments of Jehovah, and found that the children of Israel—having lost faith in his God and him—had settled for heady debauchery as worship at the feet of Baal... 'And it came to pass, as soon as he came nigh unto the camp, that he saw the calf, and the dancing: and Moses' anger waxed hot, and he cast the tablets out of his hands, and broke them beneath the mount...' He later returned to the foot of God and fasted for yet another forty days.

Then she read about Jesus of Nazareth walking the earth for forty days before his Ascension, and turned to her mom one morning and said, "Mom... I'm going to fast for forty days, too..."

"You sure you can do that Shaun?"

"Yes mom!" I have to... I just have to."

She reflected on her journey and her tears continued to flow freely...

"I won't lie, Shaun!" Sharon, one of her co-workers in the loans department later said to her after they found out that she had acquired a visa to go to the United States. *"I envy you... this is your opportunity to see the last of this blighted place!" Another said: "God knows how much you deserve this, Shaun. This day, I guess, was long in coming. But it's here... Just don't forget us!"*

Her tears flowed.

Why, Lord? Why? She thought. Why did I bother trying for that visa that got me here? I could have remained in at my desk at the Bank in Georgetown... I could have been the one saying to someone else, "I'm glad you got your visa... I wish it were I. I could have been the one going home to a simple house to tell my Carlton that a girl in my department went to the embassy today, and guess what? She got a visa to the United States. But I was that girl who got the visa. I am the one who felt so triumphant! —So proud! So lucky... Oh God why don't I feel so lucky now, why did I have to go to that embassy, Lord? Why?

"God, Mom!" she blurted. "This is so hard, mom. I've been trying to live a good life, but..." she shook her head.

"God's willing," her mom crooned. "God willing..."

And on her knees in her anguish as she heard the singing voice of her husband as he prepared for his job, and she was once again thinking about her journey...

That evening she looked around the house in which she lived with Carlton and his mother. In her heart she knew that soon she would be saying goodbye to the old house ... —goodbye to every hole in the roof, to every hole in the floor... —goodbye to the muddy yard, the stand pipe at the front and the dusty public road that ran by... goodbye to the latrine aback with the pit and maggots and dirty water that jumped and touched her bottoms —to the bathroom in the yard that forced her to take baths when it grew dark. She knew she would soon be saying goodbye to the poverty from which she had always fought to detangle herself. She knew too that soon she would be saying goodbye to Carlton with whom she'd been since she was only thirteen... with whom she became a woman... with whom she lost her first child... She knew however, that once she was in America things would be better for her, for Carlton, and for everyone she cared for. This was going to be her big break and through it she would lead many from a wilderness of economic bondage to America... The Promised Land.

She had indeed acquired much in America. As she knelt with her mom in her Mantua, New Jersey home, she had already been promoted at her corporate job to Senior Client Consultant, and Was a Pre-Paid Legal Services Inc. Director. So why wasn't she satisfied?

As she knelt in deepest of supplication, she had acquired many influential friends, and there were so many who wanted to be in her company; she knew influential people in the business community; she was affiliated to CABA, the Caribbean American Business Association; she was affiliated to NASBO, the National Society of American Business Owners; she was associated with the Christian Chamber... She knew powerful men —powerful women... So why? Why weren't things working out for her business?

Oh God, what is it that I'm doing wrong? Give me direction, oh Lord! —This is what I am fasting for, Lord!

And her mother crooned, "God's willing, me daughter... God willing..."

Shaun Stephenson was fasting because she was not happy in the aftermath of all her achievements and material acquisitions. She had indeed worked hard to be where she was. She had been tireless at the Blue Cross Corporation. She continued to be tireless working to build her Pre-Paid Legal Services Team. She was pushing at all ends to keep it up to speed and current... but things kept going flat; leads did not pan out, and times when she sat alone in her posh basement thinking, What am I doing wrong? Became more frequent.

And soon she thought of all that was afflicting her life —that all that had gone on in her life —the sickness of her Dad, Granddad... the rift between her and her dad and his subsequent passing persisted in affecting her, and she sighed and accepted that deep within her there was a crisis in the way she felt —spiritually starved and emotionally drained.

And soon she began a new search for answers. She launched herself into reading a number of books on personal development, consciousness, and awareness; she renewed reading the bible for new insights into truth. Once again she read, *Think And Grow*

Rich, by Napoleon Hill, and listened to CDs on transcendental philosophy. Soon she began to meditate at mornings. And it was one such morning that she heard the preacher on TV talking about the virtues of fasting and decided on that course, in the hope of recalibrating the direction of her life...

Things between my aunt and myself were very awkward for a while. One morning when it was snowing heavily she drove to the restaurant without me. The Turban was a mile or so away. I had to walk through the snow and the going was rough — tenuous: I slipped many times... fell a couple of times. I discovered that the white stuff that once looked so homely and beautiful in the idyllic cards we received from overseas wasn't so nice. I know my aunt Claudette was hurting. I was the only family member she had to help her and Uncle Gavin with making The Turban a dream realized. But I too had an American dream though I didn't know exactly what it was. I had left my job as a respected loans representative back in Guyana and came with great aspirations to the United States; I had come to America for a better life and being a waitress in The Turban was definitely not it.

It was soon going to be forty days. Shaun now experienced a deeper of sense of care, love and compassion for her family. She had returned from her father's funeral a few months ago and so much in her heart had been unresolved. No more. In her heart she made a resolution to be forgiving of others and in turn asked God to forgive her. In these, the last days of her forty-day fast she was given to smiling from somewhere deep within. In her heart her dad was truly at peace and so was she. The bitterness that once weighed heavily in her mind against her stepbrothers lifted.

Of late her tears were of joy and fulfillment; it was as though the tears she had shed at the beginning of her fast had washed the world clean. There was no more broken-hearted weeping because of all the hurt in the world. There was no more broken-hearted weeping because of all the hate in this world. There was no more broken-hearted weeping because of the selfishness in this world.

The fast was soon going to be ended and Shaun felt closer to illumination, enlightenment and spiritual awakening. There was peace, and felt enveloped in 'a knowing,' and somehow her mind was sharper.

Then on one of the last nights to the ending of her forty-day fast, she had a spiritual insight about *Myanda Solutions*, the company she had registered almost seven years ago... and in the insight she became sure of what it was going to be all about.

A lot of things were coming together in her mind and she began seeing the world with new set of eyes. She began to encounter a people to whom she connected at a deeper level. Richard Hay, author of a collection of Haikus entitled, *Out Of My Mind and Back To My Senses, Who Am I before Time Run Out,* became ingrained in her spiritual path, her old friend Stanley El also.

And then she was thinking of her life...

"Write your story, Shaun..." something whispered in her mind, and she chose not to hear that voice. As the fast neared its end, however, she heard the voice again. It was not whispering this time, but the voice was gentle: "Write your story, Shaun..."

She began to question the notion. *I am not famous*, she thought. *There's nothing about my life that's worth writing about..."*

"Write your story, Shaun!"

Maybe I should, Lord... she thought, and began to pray for guidance for such an undertaking. One morning a name came into her mind, a name clear as day. She reached for a writing pad and jotted the words, 'Faith Vs. Fate,' and knew she had been given the name of her story... one through which a little hope, enlightenment, and inspiration may be dispensed to the world.

As the final day dawned, Shaun Stephenson felt as though she walked on air. She saw the world in all of its perfection. And in everyone she saw that spark —that light that we all are made up of, and began to feel a deep care for all mankind. She felt part of a cosmic solution and knew that her mission was helping others — to be of service to her fellow man. She felt that God wanted her to bring hope to the lost, and to become a voice for the voiceless...

It became more and more evident that she had at last come face to face with whom she was. In her mind she embraced a truth: that she was created in the Image and Likeness of God. On the last day of her fast, Shaun Stephenson allowed herself to bask in the Presence. In her heart she danced in a place that she had never gone before —a place with a vibration that was harmonious and peaceful...

At the end of the long fast, Shaun did not only find the direction she sought, and knew that her life had forever been changed, and that thenceforth her life was destined to be one of gratitude and praise —giving thanks each moment for the simplest of things, seeing perfection in all and everything around her.

. . .

To show her thanks and gratitude for all who supported her throughout the forty-day intercession that ended with her becoming a vegetarian, Shaun, had a day of thanksgiving at her Mantua, New Jersey home. Reverend Tony C. Evans led the gathering, and Bruce, her good friend and associate, did the catering. It was a time of sharing. Everyone present spoke of enlightening, personal experiences, and the atmosphere was one of peace and harmony.

. . .

I came off my fast knowing that nothing was impossible —that I was going to move forward in belief —doing good and being of Service, with a commitment to helping others to know that we are our brothers' keeper... helping others to know that we are all one and have come from one source... helping others to find their inner wisdom... knowing the greatest virtue is Love.

EPILOGUE: 2007

Faith Vs. Fate

HOLDING FAST TO A PRE-PAID LEGAL DREAM

Shaun rubber-banded the last deck of business cards; laid them back before the printer off the sides of the flat screen monitor, and sighed in muted exasperation. She had been hoping to find the business card that Woodbury Councilwoman, Gwendolyn Brown had given her at a recent Health Fair. She had promised to get back to the councilwoman, was ready to do so, but could not find the envelope was onto which she had jotted the telephone number.

She breathed calmly, and swiveled in her chair to face the wall with her dream board of daily, short and long-term goals. At the base of it were half-opened reams of paper and a few stacks of Pre-Paid Legal Services brochures. Next to one of the stacks was a plastic file box with a lid that was at the back her SUV two days ago. *I brought this in with me yesterday...* she thought. She sighed and shook her head. "Yes," she whispered "I had this with me when I was sorting the mail... and then the phone rang..."

She chuckled to herself and went over to the box, opened the lid and there was the letter from the mortgage company and there was Gwendolyn Brown's phone number scribbled in purple.

She went back to her huge desk that was horseshoe-shaped and made of heavy glass. She made the call, and got a voice mail, left a message and hung up. She swiveled to her left, reached for the wafer sticks she would inadvertently munch on while working in her basement office, and her eyes fell on an old brochure, *Ethnic Expressions, home Gallery.*

"I couldn't find this," she said, then remembered that her mom, before leaving for church this morning, had called up to her room to say that she had left something or other in the office. Shaun picked up the hand worn thing...

The low humming of the furnace came in to her along with the seemingly distant screaming of a metal singer from her neighbor's house. Shaun felt the texture of the old catalog below her fingers. On the cover of it, there was an ebonite vase with large, white roses on a mahogany dresser. Over from the vase was a figurine of a young, Black girl... head up... eyes closed, and it seemed as though she was deeply inhaling a fragrant future. Between the vase and figurine lay an open bible. On the wall above the arrangement was a painting of an elegant Black woman, seemingly frozen at that moment of turning after having heard her name called.

"This too shall pass..." Shaun Stephenson whispered. It was the name of the sizable Andre' Thompson print.

Breathing carefully, she opened the old catalog and looked at the Fred Matthews painting, *A Gift From God,* and remembered the first time she had seen it, and how it had affected her...

. . .

She pulled into the parking lot of Jordan's on Sicklerville Road, Sicklerville, New Jersey, and got out of her Explorer. She hoped that Pat, her hairdresser, might be able to freshen up her hair in time for her to make that 3: P.M. appointment she had with a Pastor at Wegman's in Mount Laurel, after which she had to be at a networking event hosted by the Metropolitan, Trenton, African American, Chamber Of Commerce.

She entered the salon and hairdresser/proprietor Pat McRae, tall —elegant was behind the counter with one of her assistants tending to some paper work. "You're here, Shaun," she said without looking up.

"Hi, girlfriend," Shaun said cheerfully.

"No one under the sink, no one under the dryer right now —I'm in luck..."

"You are..." Pat said absently as she flipped the page of the invoice before her. "Another girlfriend of mine just left..."

"I'm glad, because I have a few appointments I don't want to be late for, the earliest one is at three..."

"I'll be finished with you long before that... I'll be with you in a minute..."

"Oh wow!"

"Shaun... what are you 'oh-wowing' about?"

"That painting..." Shaun was looking off to the wall on her right.

"Oh, that..."

"My God!" Shaun said and went over for a closer look.

. . .

She sat in her basement office and closed her eyes. "Maybe if I had a child, things might have turned out differently," she whispered.

She remembered...

The painting on the Salon's wall was entitled, *A Gift From God.* It showed a pair of careful hands—a woman and a man's—gently holding a baby between their touching palms.

"Oh, my God, Pat!" Shaun gushed.

"Shaun, you okay?" Pat asked with a little laugh.

"I just love this piece, Pat! —You don't know how much this means to me..."

"I know, Shaun... I know..." the hairdresser said and closed the huge supplies catalog she had been marking up. "I'm ready for you, girl..."

Shaun stepped beyond the counter and sat in the chair. From that vantage point she saw yet another painting that took her breath away. It was entitled, *Step Out In Faith,* and it showed a blindfolded woman stepping off a cliff below where troubled waters waited. Shaun looked closer, and discerned an invisible hand open to catch the woman should she fall.

"Are those for sale, Pat?" she blurted. "Can I have them?"

"Yes, Shaun... they're for sale—"

" I hope no one has bought them yet! —What's the cost for them? —I must have these two paintings..."

"They're prints..."

"Can I have them?"

"Calm yourself, Shaun," she said. "I don't think they're on reserve for anyone..."

"How can you know for sure?"

"I'll call the girl who sells them and find out..." Pat picked up her cell phone and began thumbing digits...

Shaun sat in her basement office and remembered...

Pat got through to the contact, and gave Shaun a price for the pieces after hanging up. Shaun wrote a check, and loaded the pair of prints into the back of her Explorer after her hair was done.

That afternoon, she picked up, author Richard Hay and Rap entrepreneur, DJ Juice—both of whom were taking work to display at the event—and headed to the Chamber networking event in Trenton. In the back of the vehicle were a few cases of *The Source*, a new brand of water she was going to help its producer promote, along with the pair of paintings that had been destined for her basement.

At last she pulled into the parking lot of the Marriott Hotel, Trenton, and began taking stuff out of the Explorer, Shaun heard a clear voice in her head. "Those paintings that you just bought," it said. "Present them to the Chamber."

What's going on in my mind? She thought. *I can't give them away! I just bought these for myself!*

This was during her forty-day fast —a time when she was beginning to be more and more in tune with a higher consciousness, and thought she should listen to inner voices, and it came again:

"Present them to the Chamber, Shaun. They were given to you so that you may give..."

She turned and told Richard and DJ to take the pair of paintings in to the hall with the rest of her stuff, and when she entered and saw John Harmon, President and CEO of the Chamber, she said to him, "John, all this stuff I have brought—including the art—is for the Chamber. It's up to you to decide what you're going to do with it.

She remembered how thankful and appreciative he had been.

The Chamber, subsequently, held an auction, and the pair of paintings was one of the items up for bidding.

She remembered...

As she sat there and saw her art on display, she prayed that whomever got them would be tremendously blessed. In her heart she knew that whomever was destined to get them would be blessed just as she was when she first saw them.

The auction started, and soon the print with the hands with the baby was being bidden on. At the event there was a doctor who was being honored that night, and she seemed bent on acquiring the piece. With her were her husband and their little girl. The price of the print kept going higher and higher, and Shaun was silently thrilled. The doctor made the winning bid for *A Gift From God;* it was an impressive figure. The piece was finally hers.

The other painting, *Step Out In faith,* also went for a very decent price.

Shaun sat in her basement office and remembered...

She later learned that it was presented to a woman in the audience who was suffering from cancer, but whose faith had kept her alive.

Shaun remembered...

As she sat at the auction she felt moved to tell the story of why she donated the pair of pictures that she had fallen in love with. She got John Harmon's attention, she told him that she wanted to speak, and he was happy to have her accommodated.

Lori Wilson, the Master Of ceremonies, mistakenly introduced her as the Artist.

"Ladies and gentlemen... I am not he artist —I wish I were...

"I am truly Blessed and grateful to all of you tonight for allowing me a few minutes of your time to share the story behind the pictures...

"I stand before you tonight filled with joy... because I followed my heart and donated them to the Chamber...

"I have not too long ago, come off a forty-day fast, and it was the most enlightening and awakening time of my life... I speak to you tonight as a child of God tonight letting you know, that no matter who your are or where you are, or what's going on in your life, God's got a plan for us all... As such, we need not be afraid to step out, like the woman in the picture, and follow your dreams...

"If you look closely, you'll see the hand outstretched from out of the clouds...

"Like this woman, I have made a step off a cliff, and I am being borne aloft by the Grace of God, and my faith and belief in my dreams... And I know that they will come through because it

is not about me, but about being of Service to mankind and helping us all step out in faith...

"The picture with the baby touched me because I've had seven
miscarriages...

"I am still childless... —but I hope and pray that the person
that now owns this picture is now blessed by my willingness to
give them over. I had bought them for myself but afterwards gave
them away by some sort of divine prompting... —it's the only way
that I can put it...

"I am truly blessed and grateful to all of you tonight for allowing me a few minutes of your time... Let's all endeavor to be more
loving and caring to each other. Thank you and God Bless..."

She remembered...

In the ensuing silence there were tears being shed across the
room.

Shaun sat in her basement office and remembered that after
the gala had ended, the Doctor who had acquired, *A Gift From
God,* approached and hugged her, then introduced her daughter,
Princess who had been born premature and was so tiny could
have fitted between her and her husband's palms.

"Shaun," the Doctor said almost in tears, "my husband would have
paid whatever it cost for it... Thank you... thank you so much..."

"Thank you for the opportunity to be a part of your life," Shaun
said —she too in tears.

She remembered...

The Doctor took a picture with Shaun, with little Princess in
between.

Quite a few people said how touched they were —how inspired.
There were those, however, who asked, "Why didn't you tell that
story *before* the auction? They would have gone for more money."

Shaun shook her head. "It's not about the money," she whispered. "It's never because of the money..."

Shaun Stephenson stood hugging herself on the deck of her
Mantua home. The snow covered the driveway that opened up
past the mailbox, and onto Berkley road on her right. To her
left... the snow covered the sturdy picnic table and every bit of
ground between it and the storage shed and between that and
everything —stretching towards the covered pool. She turned a
little and looked over the snow-covered ground where Carlton

used to plant his mammoth garden of cabbages, spinach, and a variety of callaloo... Eggplant, zucchini... tomatoes... lettuce... you name it, Carlton planted it during those years when her love for him was as fresh... as green. In her mind's eye she saw him stopped in his sleeveless vest and shorts... with his gardening trowel in his hand... with the light glinting off his joyful sweating in the yard of their home...

For the last twelve months the garden, like the pool that saw so much fun, was no more. It was gone like Carlton was gone.

She sighed... hugged herself.

She heard the screen to the kitchen door behind her. It was her mother who was on vacation from her live in job in Bernardsville.

"Shaun, girl... what you doing out in that cold, eh?"

"It's not really cold, ma..." she answered without looking back.

"But what you doing out there alone? You trying to be one of those Eskimo people?"

Shaun laughed. "I'm okay, I'm not cold. I have on my coat..."

"Okay..." Her mom said and withdrew.

As the flurries came, her emotions welled up as she thought of her husband. The truth was he did not leave her; the truth was that it was *she* who asked him to leave. She felt that his aura of doubt had begun affecting her very life. Their differences had grown so acute that she had left the matrimonial bedroom and began sleeping in the guest room.

She sighed and brushed a snowflake from the tip of her nose. *It's so hard to accept that my marriage is broken,* she thought.

"But is it?" she whispered. "Is it really broken? Maybe we needed to be apart for a while. Who knows? Maybe our being apart is our healing... maybe us being apart will help us to truly connect with ourselves... Maybe us being apart was destined buy fate... maybe our being apart will brings us back together..."

As she stood thinking out in the snow, however, she did not wonder about the path she had taken. Despite the fact that members of the very team she had built seemed to have lost faith in Pre-Paid Legal and were moving back to safer things.

Shaun Stephenson, however, stood resolute in her belief that all the groundwork she had laid would soon pay dividends would vindicate what had become her life... She was confident that all she had done and was continuing to do as a Pre-Paid Legal Services Independent Associate was destined to vindicate the uncountable hours she spent on the road —meeting people, doing presentations... and denying herself her life as a wife...

She thought of many Associates who had long given up on the business, and gone back to prior jobs that seemed sure. Most said that they had kids to feed. Shaun understood. If she had children, she surmised, maybe she too might have given up and went back to Blue Cross... or maybe not.

Maybe God did not give me children for a reason...

She sighed and thought of her seven miscarriages. *Maybe God made me childless so that I can go out there and make a difference in the lives of countless others... Maybe...*

She sighed and brushed a snowflake from her upper lip. In the background she heard the muted snarl of a metal rock musician coming from her neighbor's house.

A snowplough clattered by.

She had finally received monies that were due her from her former job, and things had begun to change for the better. She had always known that her life was going to change for the better because Universal Law does not change.

She had always whispered, "God will help me —once *I* take action, or there's no God!"

Shaun Stephenson looked out into whiteness and was content. Deep in her heart the heralding light of good things to come her way was rivaled only by the whiteness of the snow about her.

A light breeze ruffled her hair.

She remembered the calm that had overtaken her when she emerged into America from the JFK airport. It *was* destined to be the symbolical stillness before a storm of new experiences that subsequently came her way. In her mind, however, there had been a sigh of relief after the many years of struggle and pain and hope she had left behind...

And here she stood in Mantua, New Jersey after a journey of fourteen years of struggle and pain and hope in America.

And in her heart of hearts she knew that through all that she has gone through —that through all that she was destined to go through... there would always be her faith.

ACKNOWLEDGEMENTS

The Highest honor and praise I give to my Creator —The Invincible Presence of God without whom I can do nothing. It is through *God in Action* directing my path on this journey called life, that I have been allowed to connect with the following individuals whom I can only describe as gracious, and to whom I say, a heartfelt "Thank you!" for being a part of my continuing journey: To Mr. Harland Stonecipher, CEO and Founder of Pre-Paid Legal Services Incorporated who graciously permitted me to use an excerpt from his inspirational Las Vegas 2006 speech; to Rev. Tony C. Evans Sr., who saw my light and encouraged me to walk by Faith and take Action from the first time we met; to Jackie Jennifer who always told me *I can!* and is always there to listen; to Brenda Musgrove, my sister in Christ, and Pastor Donald Medley whose words of inspiration help my journey; to Tammy Grove, my sister in spirit, who continues to stand in support; to my Aunt Bridget who's support got me through many difficult parts of my journey. I also say 'Thank You' to: Monica McGill, Sharome Wade, Shannon Sharp, Andrea Panico, Jonah Cooper, Kenneth Evans, Patricia McRae, Carlette Southern-Roberts, Sheri Desatrez, and Sue Urda of Powerful You!, Debra P. Dilorenzo, Mel Zimmerman, Sharon Addison, Rory Wells, Brian Short (DJ Juice), Audrey Bell, Richard Hay who—before I met the author—had volunteered to write this story. I also extend gratitude to Stanley El, my Beloved brother of the light, Mr. David Allen, my Pre-Paid Legal Coach and his PPLSI team, Maryetta Marks, Zonia Warchala, Jenell Tomlinson and everyone on Phenomenal Women for Justice Team. Special thanks to Christina Edwards for her energy, enthusiasm and unconditional support, to Damali Bascom who so believed in this project offered unconditional financial support, to my biographer, novelist/playwright Harold Bascom who tirelessly labored on this project and brought it to life with his insights and creativity. On behalf of Mr. Bascom and myself, I extend a sincere 'Thank

You' to the following readers who volunteered to go through the bound manuscript before we went to press: Ms. Orienthia Rickets, Prof. Maurice Sampson, Rev. Tony C. Evans Sr., Mr. Carlton Stephenson, Ms. Zonia Warchala, Mr. David Smile, Mr. David Allen, Ms. Christina Edwards, Dr. Phyllis Adams, Ms. Desiree McPherson, Ms. Gwendolyn Brown, Ms. Loreen Howard, Ms. Damali Bascom, and Mr. Richard Hay.

I am sure there are many wonderful individuals whom I have not mentioned but who continue to enhance my journey meaningfully. You know yourselves, and to you, also, I am forever grateful.

—*Shaun Stephenson.*

ABOUT THE AUTHOR

Harold A. Bascom—a prize-winning playwright/dramatist, and Heinemann Caribbean Writers Series novelist—was born in Guyana, South America. He is also a book illustrator; fine artist, graphic designer, and independent publisher. About his talents he contends modestly: "Below all of that, I am just a social observer."

In the winter of 2007 Shaun Stephenson approached him with the idea for a book project: her story. He said 'yes' and so began a literal challenge of love.

About the mixed literary format he has incorporated into the manuscript —part fictionalized and shifting from first person to third person narratives, and part actual interview script: "I always felt the need to write as if I'm doing a mixed media painting where there is an area made up of collage, another painted with oils, another with water colors, another in pen and ink —you know, that kind of freedom to be creative —to do something as Anthony Burgess did with language; to do something as James Joyce did with prose —to write without fear of censure." As such, he rates *Faith vs. Fate* as one of the more exciting projects he has thus far tackled as a writer.

Bascom lives in Hackensack, New Jersey.